Prisoner From Beyond the River

Also by Geoffrey Bull

WHEN IRON GATES YIELD

GOD HOLDS THE KEY

CORAL IN THE SAND

THE SKY IS RED

TIBETAN TALES

A NEW PILGRIM'S PROGRESS

THE CITY AND THE SIGN

LOVE-SONG IN HARVEST

For younger readers

I AM A DONKEY

I AM A FISH

I AM A PUPPY

I AM A MOUSE

I AM A LAMB

I AM A SPARROW

Prisoner From Beyond the River

by

GEOFFREY T. BULL

HODDER AND STOUGHTON

LONDON SYDNEY AUCKLAND TORONTO

Contents

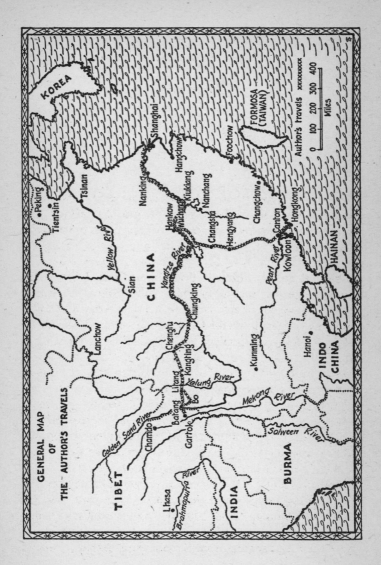

GENERAL MAP
OF
THE AUTHOR'S TRAVELS

Author's travels xxxxxxxxx

Miles
0   100   200   300   400

KOREA

Peking
Tientsin

Tsinan

Shanghai
Nanking
Hankow
Wuchang
Kiukiang
Nanchang
Hangchow

FORMOSA (TAIWAN)

Foochow

Yellow River

Sian

CHINA

Yangtze River

Changsha
Hengyang

Changchow

Canton
Hongkong
Kowloon

HAINAN

Lanchow

Chengtu
Kangting

Chungking

Kunming

Hanoi

INDO CHINA

Yalung River

Litang
Batang
Bo

Golden Sand River

Chamido
Gartok

Mekong River

Solween River

BURMA

TIBET

Lhasa
Brahmaputra River

River

INDIA

CHAPTER I

Lizards Are Lovely

ONCE UPON A TIME (that, of course, is how all the best stories begin), I was born in the city of London. My parents (who were delighted to have me!) told me just when it was: June the twenty-fourth, nineteen twenty-one, so my birthday is on Midsummer's Day. Now that I am supposed to be older (which is rather different from being old) I forget the candles and just eat the birthday cake! Still, I am not so old that I cannot remember what I did as a boy and how I grew up and went as a missionary to far-off lands. In fact, I wrote my story in a book called *When Iron Gates Yield*, but as some of the words were rather long and the number of pages a trifle too many, I'm going to tell it all over again with you younger people in mind.

As my story is a true one and just a bit frightening, you'll have to be brave if you are coming along. We are going to the Land of Tibet, that mysterious kingdom that lies beyond Mount Everest on the 'roof of the world'. We shall watch out for bandits beyond the ranges and across the wind-swept grasslands; and we shall camp with the nomads and live in a log cabin, where the smoke gets in your eyes. We shall meet strange characters, like Azung, the crazy lama and the ninth general of the Tibetan Army, with his long, blue ear-ring dangling from his ear. And perhaps I should warn you, we'll get captured by the Chinese Communist Army far away in the mountains. There's a whole crowd of folk I'd like you to meet, but most of all, the Friend who rescued me. Still I think you'll agree, we must start at the beginning or we'll be spoiling the story.

The first thing I remember is paddling on the beach. I was barely three then but I still think it's a lovely feeling, taking off your shoes and socks and racing across the sands to the sea. The second thing I remember, is my lizard. It was quite small and black all over. It would wriggle and jerk in my clammy wee hand but I thought it was beautiful. One night it escaped and got through the fence into next-door's garden. Sad to say, the lady who lived there managed to catch it, and you'd hardly believe it, but she cut it in half with a pair of scissors!

Our own back-garden was a splendid place and seemed very big to me, though, of course, the smallest place looks big when you are small yourself. We had two large cherry trees. I loved the cherries — but so did the birds! We had an apple tree too. My grandfather fell off a ladder once, when he was picking the apples. Another thing was the sandpit. I liked to play in it especially when the new sand came. It was so clean and yellow. On one occasion I tried to help do the gardening but I pulled up the bulbs, those flaky 'onions' that grow into tulips and 'things'! After that my mother thought I should leave it to her, and needless to say, I didn't object.

When I was five we moved away to the other side of London. It was quite an adventure. We went to a new housing-estate in the middle of the fields. There was mud everywhere and at first the farmer's cows came into our back-yard. Then I went to school down in the village. I hated it and cried quite a lot the first day but I got used to it in the end; and I think after a while, they even got used to me! I also went to church on Sundays. Our Sunday school was the biggest in all England (or nearly the biggest). Over a thousand children went to it. Most of them had moved out of the poor parts of London to nice new homes in the suburbs. I began to hear about Jesus in those days and how we all ought to become Christians. One day, I believe I became one and Jesus came into my heart. Later on, I asked him to come in more properly — just to make sure.

At school one morning, my teacher tried to find out what we wanted to be when we grew up. Those were the days of the old-fashioned bi-planes, big clumsy airships and cheap second hand cars. It was as much as anybody could do to get off the ground, and as for the moon, it was still very far away. Boys longed to be engine-drivers on the steam trains you never see today; and girls didn't want to be anything much but stayed at home with their mothers until they got married! When it came up to my turn, I blurted out something that no-one expected.

'I want to be a missionary,' I said.

I was no more than ten then, but some fifteen years later, that's exactly what happened. And if you are good at mental arithmetic you will know now, just how old I was when I went to China and Tibet.

CHAPTER 2

Butter-Lamp House

GEORGE, A VERY BRAVE Scotsman, and I, a not so brave Englishman, arrived in Shanghai in the Spring of 1947. What a place it proved to be! Thousands of people everywhere, shops covered with Chinese writing, men pulling rickshaws, cries and yells, sights and smells, and a thousand-and-one things besides. It was like a big pile of jig-saw pieces all waiting to be sorted out. We only stayed a week in the port and then caught a boat up the broad muddy waters of the Yangtze River into inland China.

The night we left Shanghai, another missionary came to see us off. On the quay the coolies were carrying heavy loads hung from bamboo poles, slung across their shoulders. They sang as they loaded the ship and the haunting sound came softly through the porthole to our little group sitting in the cabin. It was a big moment for us. Childhood days were left behind but all I had hoped for, was happening now. We were going to tell the Chinese and Tibetan people how God loved them and sent His Son, the Lord Jesus Christ to be their Saviour. We had a little prayer before we said good-bye and then all at once another song fell on our ears. Our missionary friend had begun to sing in his beautiful voice, some words which just expressed how we felt about Jesus.

King of my life I crown Thee now,
Thine may the glory be!
Lest I forget Thy thorn-crowned brow,
Lead me to Calvary.

You should have seen us some months later in the wilds of West China. We no longer travelled by boat or even by bus. We were on horseback . . . We had been in the saddle from early morning, but now night had fallen and all was pitch black. The rocky trail fell steeply away to the dark swirling waters of a wide river, called the Tung Ho. Our horses moved slowly forward, head to tail. Loshay, our horseman, led us in silence along the ledge. One false step and any one of us would have fallen headlong to the depths below. Suddenly we rounded a cliff and there, across the river, shone the friendly lights of a Chinese town. How could we reach it? The only bridge was a number of thin wire-ropes and a footway of narrow, wooden boards suspended fifty feet above the water. It stretched, we reckoned, some eighty metres through the gloom to the farther bank. Should we dare to take the horses over?

George went first with the best animal we had. It was an intelligent horse, perhaps more intelligent than us! Loshay chose to go next with our 'cheapest' horse, which we called 'The Gebo', a Tibetan word meaning 'the agéd one'. This was a harmless creature that plodded on faithfully over the miles but now, in the inky blackness, it plodded just ten short paces onto the bridge and down it went, straight through the boards! There was an awful shout from Loshay and the struggling horse sent the bridge rocking from side to side. I thought they would both topple into the river.

Just at that moment a little boy with a tiny lamp came to see what had happened. By its flickering light I tip-toed out towards Loshay and the old grey mare. What I saw made

my hair stand on end. The fat, furry 'tummy' of the Gebo
was resting on three small boards and its four shaggy legs
were dangling helplessly in space! The situation was des-
perate. Loshay pulled at its bridle and I pulled at its tail.
How its bones or muscles worked I didn't know; its tail was
bent nearly ninety degrees to its back. 'No! No!' cried
Loshay, despairingly. He thought I was snapping it off!

Little by little we heaved the frantic creature to a higher
position but then as soon as its front legs were free, they
started going like pistons. One kick and the boy with the
lamp would have been knocked in the river, not to speak of
Loshay and myself. The fearful death awaiting us in the
waters below didn't bear thinking about!

Then all at once it happened. The horse mounted the
footway and within fifteen minutes we were all safely across.
It was little short of a miracle, when you think of all those
spaces between the boards and that ghastly length of
bridge! And remember — a horse has four feet, not two!
Still, even a Gebo, I suppose, can learn by experience!

After many months of travel, and studying Tibetan as we
moved from place to place, we arrived at last at a remote
mountain village. There it lay, tucked away behind the
ranges in one of the loveliest valleys in the world. The local
people called it Bo and they lived by planting barley, tend-
ing their cattle on the hills and weaving their own cloth, all
hundreds of miles from the outside world. Most of the
peasants lived in flat-roofed houses, that looked like forts,
whilst at the head of the valley lived the 'lord of the manor'
in his big white castle. He had his own soldiers and re-
tainers and nobody was allowed to leave the valley without
his permission. He ran things along similar lines to the
feudal system which you learn about at school; but I must
say he was a kind man and gave us a great welcome among
his people. In the village by the millstream, stood a snug

little log-cabin. We rented this for a big square bundle of tea-leaves, something worth quite a bit to a Tibetan. Then we unsaddled our horses and moved in.

On the floor of the log-cabin was a stone hearth, where we lit a fire. The walls were made of long, rough tree trunks but there was only one window, which meant it was rather dark inside. After sundown our only light was a butter-lamp so we read very little in the evenings; and as for the smoke, it got into our eyes, turned our books yellow and left tar on the beams, being quite unwilling to find the hole specially made for it in the wattle roof!

It was hardly a palace but the place, we felt, where God would have us be, and this was surely, the best place of all.

CHAPTER 3

The Golden Sand River

OUR FIRST WEEKS IN Bo were like a dream — frosty mornings, glorious sunshine and rocky crags, whose crystal fingers stabbed sharply at the bright blue sky. It was all so peaceful but sometimes a messenger would come in through the mountains, bring news of the civil war still raging in China. One side was led by the Nationalist, Chiang, and the other by the Communist, Mao.* It had been going on for years but because it was fought mostly in the north, we didn't think much about it when we came to Shanghai. Now, however, the Communists were winning battle after battle. They had taken over most of China and were beginning to look westwards to Tibet. Central Asia was vital to them. If you look at a map you will see what I mean. Tibet is between Russia, India and China; and China wanted to get in there first and take the country over.

The Chieftain of Bo valley, who lived in the castle, was called Pangda. He and his brother, Rapga, wondered what the outcome would be if Mao sent his armies to conquer Tibet. All the borders would be a battlefield. We began to talk of these things and think of ways to get help to our friends.

Away to the west the ancient trails ran out across the

* i.e. Chiang Kai Shek and Mao Tse Tung.

barren wastes to the Golden Sand River. This was the name of the Yangtze in this part of its course. Beyond that river lay the towns of Gartok and Chamdo, and still further west, the little known city of Lhasa, the capital of Tibet for hundreds of years.

About this time we wrote to the Government of Tibet and asked if we could cross the Golden Sand River and enter their territory. Along its banks stood the Tibetan Army, ready to fight the Chinese Communists whenever they came. We hoped before anything like this could happen, to get into Tibet and tell the Buddhists about the Lord Jesus. George had another plan, too. He felt if one of us could cross south-east Tibet to India, then we might be able to get help for the Tibetans there and bring in some medicines for the wounded. He fondly hoped that the British and Indian Governments might also support the Tibetans; but as things turned out, this was never to be.

One night, after 'the sun had struck the passes', as the Tibetans say, Pangda and Rapga called us over to see them. The castle in which they lived had three storeys. We went through the great wooden doors on the ground floor, where the grain was stored. Then we passed on up the broad staircase, where, from the wall, hung skins of leopard, tiger, wolf and fox.

On the second floor there was a shrine and a large feudal kitchen. Sometimes a party of Buddhist priests, dressed in their long red robes, would come to frighten away demons with a band of drums and trumpets. The noise was frightful and I doubt if the demons were very impressed. In the kitchen the soldiers and servants gathered round a huge, log fire and a big, black cauldron that was hanging from the ceiling. We left them to their laughter and chatter and climbed still higher to the topmost floor. There the ruling families had their quarters.

Pangda's place was a fine roomy area, brightened with colourful cushions placed on a low platform by the window. He was exceedingly wealthy, with many cattle on the hills and untold treasures in his fortress-home. At the clap of his hands, servants would come running in to ask what he wanted. When we arrived, we sat down with Pangda and Rapga and were served, according to custom, with some buttered tea. Outside, under the stars, stretched a roof-top courtyard, where, on special feast days, the girls of the village were invited to dance in their beautiful clothes.

People travelled far and wide to visit Pangda. He advised them on their troubles and settled their quarrels. When one valley stole cattle from another, they would bring the case to him. He was asked to be the judge. Then his room was like a law court; and what he decided, they were willing to accept.

We wondered why Pangda and his brother should call us from our little log cabin to see them this night, in the great big castle. They quickly told us. A letter had come for us from the Lhasa Government beyond the river. We hastily broke the wax seal and peered together at the writing. It looked as if some fly had dipped its six spindly legs in the ink and walked across the page. But the brothers helped us to translate it.

As we listened, we recognised how wonderfully our God had answered prayer. One of us could go, it said, across the Golden Sand River to Gartok inside Tibet. In that town there lived a famous prince who was the Governor of all South East Tibet. He would now arrange for some of his soldiers to escort us through his country to the Indian frontier, several weeks journey away. Very few Christian missionaries had ever been allowed into Tibet so we felt rather excited and very grateful to God. Soon we said good night to the brothers and by the light of a flare, made our way, back to the cabin and our rough plank beds. The thing now was, who should it be?

As the butter-lamp flickered out and the embers of the fire died away, this was the question that burned in our hearts.

CHAPTER 4

A Spy Looks In

OUR GREY HORSE WAS a beauty and the day George departed for India, he rode it down the valley until we reached the point where we must say good-bye. It had proved his honour to go ahead into Tibet and my privilege to stay. He now changed mounts and I was left in charge of this fiery but excellent animal which he handled so well. How I would ride it myself, I did not know. He was its master. I doubt if I ever had sat on its back.

I stood watching George and Loshay till they disappeared down the long valley and the clip-clop of the hooves could be heard no more. To the south and the west I could glimpse the distant trail, slashed up through the pine-woods, heading out across the pass to the Golden Sand River. How I longed to tread that road, the road to Tibet; but my turn would come later. Meanwhile I must master the grey, and that was quite something! The Tibetans would just laugh at me until I did.

Day after day I took the horse out and practised my riding. If he ran too fast and began to frighten me, then I'd pray hard, pull at his head and gallop up the hillside. An angle of forty-five degrees soon slowed him down. God made horses, as well as their riders, and if ever a horse was conquered by prayer, it was the grey!

It was rather lonely in the cabin now without George, but a Tibetan boy called Gaga stayed with me and helped me with the odd jobs and the learning of the language. Being the only European for many miles around, I got to know the villagers extremely well. When they were ill they came to me and, although I was not a proper doctor, I'd learned how to give injections and to sew up wounds, so had a bit more to give than the old missionary treatment of aspirins for all above the waist and Epsom salts for everything below.

Folk came crowding to the cabin and at evening time some neighbours would gather round our open fire and spluttering butter-lamp, to hear the record-player. A 'gramophone' we called it in those days! It was always a mystery to them how the songs were sung by 'that man in the box'. There they would sit with their dirty faces and long untidy hair, crouched low in their sheepskins, drinking in the music. Gaga learned to change the records. He was very proud about this and now and then, he even changed the needle, but that wasn't often for we had so few. At such times I felt very near to these rugged people and when a Gospel singer sang some hymn I knew, I felt like singing the old lines with him:

> *I'd rather have Jesus than silver or gold,*
> *I'd rather have Jesus than riches untold,*
> *I'd rather have Jesus than houses or lands,*
> *I'd rather be led by His nail-pierced hands,*
>
> *Than to be a king of a vast domain*
> *And be held in sin's dread sway.*
> *I'd rather have Jesus than anything*
> *This world affords today.*

New Year in Bo was simply tremendous. The Tibetans certainly know how to enjoy themselves. For days they were getting ready. All the men had to have a new shirt. They wear only one a year so it does get a bit dirty! Then the women look out their dancing clothes. They make colourful blouses and new top-boots with curled-up toes. Weddings are the order of the day! The barley beer has to be brewed and the popcorn heated. The horses are fed on tea-leaves to make them fierce and the young men get set for the annual race up the mountain.

It was while all these preparations were going on, that a servant came again, one night, from the big white house, to say I must go and see Pangda. We picked our way by the light of blazing pine-chips across the now familiar court-yard. The eyes of the hunting dogs shone green in the light, and it wasn't long before I was up the three flights of stairs and seated beside the brothers. It was a letter from George. He had arrived safely in Gartok and was staying with the Prince, and what is more, the Prince had sent me a special letter, saying I could cross the Golden Sand River, too, whenever I wished.

New Year came. The local lama, a Buddhist priest who knew nothing of the living God and His love to men, kept the villagers mumbling prayers and worshipping idols. Maybe he thought he would lose his 'flock' if I talked to them about Jesus, so he got busy too. As New Year approached he called all the village together for a large religious gathering around a great big bonfire. The people made little images out of barley flour, mixed with tea and butter, and when at last the blowing of trumpets and the clanging of cymbals ceased, he lit the bonfire. The people then laid their images in front of the fire and hoped that the demons wouldn't worry them for another year. It was pitiful to see them for the whole thing was so absurd yet it was what they believed.

Then something terrible happened. There was a fearful wind that day and, as the bonfire reached its height, sparks blew from the fire into the hayricks on the flat-roofed housetops. The flames devoured them, then spread in fury to the homes below. They burned like a furnace. Most of the people were out in the fields but sadly, one woman was caught in the blaze and was almost burned to death. I looked after her for many weeks until she was better, but even then, I had to cut off one of her fingers, which was black as cinder.

In a new room built on the side of the log cabin, I hung Bible posters. There was one showing a sower at work in his field. There was one of the father welcoming home his prodigal son and there was another with three crosses, a whip, some nails and a crown of thorns. These were pictures of the stories that Jesus told and a reminder of how He suffered for us on the Cross. There was also a text of Scripture in Tibetan. I was hoping to reach the people not only by dressing their wounds but with the message of the Gospel, before I went to Tibet itself.

Meanwhile news from China grew worse and worse. The Communist armies were now only two weeks riding away. I felt maybe I ought to get moving. Then one day, while I was away up country visiting nearby Batang, down through the forest came a small party of Chinese troops, and six of them set up camp in the village of Bo. It was quite dangerous for them, of course, living amongst the Tibetans, with their supporting forces still well to the rear, but the Pangda brothers dare not make them prisoners or allow the Tibetans to kill them, as it was now certain that the Chinese Communists were coming, and revenge would be swift.

One morning one of the Communist officers in his yellow uniform came marching over to the log-cabin. I was not unduly afraid because they were too few and I knew they dare not touch me in this remote village, where I was loved and respected by the people.

'You are a deceiver,' the man said to me. 'You cheat the people.'

'A few years under Communism and we shall know who has cheated the people,' I replied. Then I began to talk to him about the Lord Jesus and turned him to a verse in a Chinese Gospel of John. 'This is the condemnation,' it read, 'that light is come into the world and men love darkness rather than light because their deeds are evil.' He tried to change the subject and pointing to my typewriter, asked rudely, 'Is that a wireless transmitter?' Finally he left with four Chinese Gospels in his pocket but feeling, I'm sure, that I was some secret agent of the British Government.

Later on I found pieces of the Gospels torn up and thrown into the open-air toilet at the foot of the courtyard. I was beginning to see what the Communists think of God and the gift of His Son. I was sorry about it but what could I do? Should I stay any longer? Gaga and I began to prepare secretly for the dash to Tibet across the mountains to the Golden Sand River. Once across the frontier, an officer of the Tibetan Army would meet us at an arranged point and take us to the Prince at Gartok, eighty miles inside Tibet.

One day soon after sunrise, I opened the cabin door and looked towards the Communist camp. God was working a miracle. The Chinese were dismantling their aerial and packing up their radio equipment. They were going to pull out. It was they who were the spies!

No sooner were they gone than Rapga announced his departure for the river and Chamdo. He was taking a message to the Lhasa Government. Pangda was staying at Bo, or at least his household was. He would try to talk to the Communists coming in from the east. He knew he could never fight them. Who was he, to take on all China? He would have to do the next best thing. Whilst Rapga was talking to Lhasa he would talk to them. Between them, who could tell, some kind of agreement might yet be worked out? It was a forlorn hope but at least he'd try.

Three days after Rapga left, Gaga and I, with a few horsemen from the village, slipped down the great ravine and headed up over the passes. The big white castle of the House of Pangda faded slowly from our view.

I never saw it again.

CHAPTER 5

Forbidden Frontier

WE CROSSED THE FIRST ridge and descended from the bare hilltop, down to where the tree-line began. The sun twinkled through the leaves and for a little while we forgot the pressure of the past weeks, living under the watchful eye of the Communist spies.

What we didn't know was that Rapga and his party of loyal Tibetan horsemen were facing a new threat as they approached the Golden Sand River. He had wondered whether he would get through without trouble and had especially said to me, that I should on no account, travel with him. He did not trust the Communists and would take no chances. His men were well armed. Few knew how powerful the brothers were in the mountains. Rapga said they could rally five thousand Tibetans against the Chinese but their weapons were not fit for the task. If Tibet did not unite or receive help from the outside world their cause was lost. He was returning to his country with a sad heart. It was almost too late to do anything now.

Whilst we were enjoying the peaceful sunshine high up in the mountains, Rapga and his party were suddenly surprised by about fifteen riders coming in from the north. In a split second rifles were at the ready and revolvers at the hip. One shot from either side and there would have been a fight to the death yet the horsemen did not fire but rode cautiously forward watching each other's movements.

Who were these 'bandits'? Rapga had a pretty good idea and was not far wrong. They were a group of underground Communists, half Tibetan and half Chinese, who were working for Mao. The spy-network had informed them in Batang (the town near to Bo not yet taken by the Chinese Armies), that Rapga was trying to escape to Tibet, so out they had come to stop him. The leader of this Communist cell in Batang was Wanjee. He now came forward and with clever talk tried to persuade Rapga not to continue. This way and that, he argued, but Rapga would not be swayed. He was going through. Rapga growing impatient signalled his party to proceed. It was a test of nerves. Unless there was a shoot-out, nothing would stop him. Wanjee backed down. He had not yet been given the authority to kill. Rapga would be too valuable to the Chinese Communists, once Tibet was in their hands. They would meet Rapga later, when the war was won. Meanwhile Wanjee's bluff had been called.

By the time we reached the spot three days afterwards, not a soul was to be seen. No one, thank God, had reported us to Wanjee. We were through. At about sixteen thousand feet we met a blizzard and camped overnight under inches of snow but the next day, out came the sun, and it melted away. The trail was dirty but not too badly affected and we began to descend the endless zig-zag path to the Golden Sand River below. It was terrific country, which few Westerners have ever seen. Through the deep canyon the waters pour and the mighty cliffs rise upward to the skies.

Once at the bottom we stood on the beach and looked a hundred metres across the terrifying current. A little village lay on the farther side. It was the place the prince had mentioned. There we were to meet his man. How we were to cross the river I was not sure but the horsemen knew the ropes. They started shouting and their voices echoed back and forth across the chasm as the sound bounced round the cliffs.

At last we saw movement on the western bank. It seemed as if two giant insects, like beetles, were creeping along the shore. You would have thought that they were prehistoric reptiles or perhaps some abominable snowmen come out to meet us. Whatever could these creatures be? They turned out to be yak-hide coracles carried upside down on two men's shoulders.

First of all they rowed their fragile craft up stream close in to the rock. Then they launched out into the eddying flow until they were swept downstream and across to where we were. They were wild-looking customers and as strong as young lions. The loads from the horses were carefully laid in one of the coracles, which floated like an eggshell on the water. The weight put it down a foot and so steadied it. 'Don't be afraid!' somebody said but I was praying as I jumped in! Down stream I could see there were rapids and we had to make the crossing before the quickening current caught us.

What about the grey? He did all right. A long leather thong was attached to his bridle and a man in the other coracle held on to it while the poor creature was forced out with sticks and stones into the deeper water. As it began to swim, the oarsmen began to row and the mad struggle to cross the river was on. The coracles were hardly more than two metres wide and stood just half a metre out of the water. It was the kind of thing, that lifts you out of your chair on the screen but shakes you to the foundations when you yourself are in the real live scene.

It was with great relief that I jumped out on the stones, safe at last, inside Tibet. The plains of China were now four hundred miles away through the mountains. I could only thank God and in good heart, press on towards Gartok.

I hardly realised how hot it was in the lower altitude until I entered the inn in the village. This was the head-quarters of the Tibetan Army, who had a small post at that part of the border. I was glad to find that the Prince had not failed us. His man was there. The inn was also a mule-teers' hostel and tough looking characters were for ever coming and going. Their main business was in salt, mined somewhere further south. They were armed to the teeth and went about their business with daggers and pistols in their belts, swearing at each other most of the time. It was like living with pirates on the Spanish Main.

That afternoon, I sat with a group of Tibetan teenagers on the beach, where I talked to them about the true God. The only god they knew was an idol so all I had to say was very new to them. They listened eagerly, surprised that I could speak their language.

At night I slept on the open roof-top of the inn and next morning the army officer, who was the Prince's man, told me that our pack horses had arrived and that we should get ready to move. By then quite a line of sick people had queued up to see me. There were many sore eyes, so I first had a medical parade and then, jumping on the grey, climbed out of the close, warm atmosphere of the valley to the keen, fresh air on the heights.

We passed through high farming country, quiet and still in the morning light, though soon to be the scene of war. Then on again, travelling from village to village, and some-times stopping in their fort-like dwellings. Along the track were piles of stones carved with Buddhist sayings. Two or three days, and we reached the military post of Hla Dun. We cantered into the tumbledown township through the pouring rain. I especially remember it for rain is a luxury in

Tibet. After another change of horses and a chat over tea with the Commanding Officer, we rode on to Ja Gag. There a pleasant surprise awaited us. Rapga and his party were resting in a big mansion, the trading station of Azung, Pangda's agent in that corner of Tibet. I had seen Azung once before when he visited Bo, dressed as a lama in gorgeous robes — though no more a lama than the man in the moon! He was quite a comedian and his whole life a game of charades. Though he looked crazy he was as sharp as a needle. This day, it would seem, was not a 'lama' day for him, so he looked like any ordinary Tibetan!

I was thrilled to meet Rapga again and to catch up with the news. It was here that I learned of their narrow escape, east of the river. We stayed some days and Azung, our host, thoroughly enjoyed himself. One day we were looking at a strange idol in the family god-room. It was the kind of thing you see in a nightmare! It had a woman's face set in a circle of arms. There were so many you could hardly count them and they were all sticking out of her neck! The effect was rather like a Catherine Wheel on bonfire night. 'Now isn't that a lovely god!' piped up Azung with a twinkle in his eye. I felt he was teasing me, so I just took the opportunity, in a quiet way, to tell him about the Lord Jesus. It was hard to know what he really believed.

At last, the day came for the final stage of our journey to Gartok, where we must meet the Prince, the Governor of South East Tibet. We were now quite a large company of riders. The horses were a fine sight in their saddle rugs and we rode in our best Tibetan robes to meet our host. As we came across a low hill, a wide grassy plain opened up before us and there, on the farther side, the Governor's fortress and the little township could be clearly seen.

News of our arrival had gone ahead of us and the whole population lined the roadside as we made our way in. We clattered up through the main archway of the fort and then, as we dismounted, the Prince came forward to meet us. He stood tall and regal in his silken gown, smiling his welcome to us all. From his ear hung a long turquoise earring, the badge of his office.

'Are you tired?' he asked kindly. 'Then come along in!'

And together we walked through the flower garden, to his restful apartments.

CHAPTER 6

Bullets Fly!

THE ROOM FROM WHICH the Prince ruled South East Tibet was very like the one from which Pangda ruled his valley. We sat down on the cheerful rugs and cushions by the window, and sipped buttered tea way into the sunset. Servants came and went, whenever the Prince clapped his hands. When after some hours of chatting together, I could hardly keep my eyes open, a servant took me to my bedroom.

After a week or two, Rapga left for Chamdo. He carried a letter asking the Lhasa Government to let me stay in Tibet, and allow George and myself to organise a medical team from India to help the Tibetans. During my stay in Gartok I explored the surrounding countryside with its low-lying hills and broad, treeless plain. The entire area lay at least fourteen thousand feet above the sea; but as most Tibetans have never seen the sea, a figure like that would mean nothing to them! I discovered that the nearest Englishman was in Chamdo, about ten days riding away. He was a Mr. Robert Ford, employed as a radio operator by the Tibetan Government. I began to wonder whether George might soon return with supplies. I was very lonely and my times talking to the Lord Jesus became more precious and real. I wondered too, what decision I should make in the dangerous situation. Should I get away before the Chinese armies reached Gartok or should I stay and try to preach to the Communists as well? It might be difficult but not impossible. God's answer, surely, would be given?

The days passed and the Prince and I taught each other more about our own languages. He could speak English, as well as I could speak Tibetan. I attended a three-day 'feast' at the magistrate's house. He was the Prince's next door neighbour; but the food was not very interesting and the games boring. Everyone's thoughts were faraway, wondering when the invasion would begin. Nearly every day news came of clashes between Tibetan and Chinese patrols. At times I stood and watched the local peasants making their crude type of paper or hammering out a silver bowl. They were paid so little for doing it and I felt sad for them and the life they lived. The rich were so rich and the poor so poor. The Prince was kind to them, though, and everybody loved him.

He had started a day school for his own three children and those of the soldiers. The Prince had a little girl of nine, a boy of seven, and also a younger boy of five. They thought the world of their father, for their mother had died. The servants gave them their food and looked after them but they were allowed to play with the other boys and girls. The Prince did not keep them apart.

I thought it strange to see how they learned their lessons. They would shout them out at the top of their voice; and I often heard them reciting Buddhist sayings across the courtyard, as I sat talking with the Prince or some of the lamas. When their lessons had been written out, the children would come, one by one, and hold up their slate for the Prince to see. They really worked quite hard. They also looked after the flowers. They carried the pots from place to place, the blooms tickling their noses. When the Prince praised them they returned to the school room, their faces full of smiles.

One night in the middle of August, the Prince and I were sitting talking in the soft glow of the butter-lamp. It was about half past nine and fully dark outside. The children were sleeping peacefully in the same room, as they liked to be where their father was. Everything was quiet and still. The lama-music, which marked the close of the day, had not yet sounded and the final cannon, a sort of 'lights out', had not been fired. Nothing seemed to move.

Then there was a violent shudder and the building rocked and creaked from end to end. We sat bolt upright, stiff and alert. Then it happened again but more powerfully this time. Clay plaster started falling from the ceiling and the wooden pillars cracked apart from the walls. It was an earthquake! Like a flash we sprang to our feet and ran for the door. We snatched the children from their rugs en route — the five year old, without a stitch of clothing on him. Helter-skelter we tumbled into the garden and staggered to the centre of the courtyard. None of us could stand for the earth was heaving. We crouched very low and waited and waited. Once things were still again we ventured indoors. Then came a new terror. Out from the star-filled sky we heard the most unearthly noises. The Tibetans were terrified and one of the servants ran quickly to the roof and lit some incense. 'The gods are fighting,' he said.

A few days later, news trickled in, telling us that in the earthquake near the Indian border, the very mountains had moved and that one of the big rivers had been blocked by falls of rock. Several people had also been killed. I came to the conclusion that the noise in the sky was the echo of this tremendous upheaval. I was told too, that the trails to India, used by George six months before, had all been destroyed.

As I thought about it all, I realised now, that God had

allowed me to be enclosed inside Tibet. He must have a purpose in it all. Maybe I *was* to stay, and be His witness to the Communists.

As the weeks went by, a strange silence settled over the Golden Sand River. The Chinese patrols grew less and less. Whatever were the Communists doing? Was this the lull before the storm? On one occasion a letter was brought in from the other side of the river. The Prince opened it and found that it was a message from Wanjee of Batang, the Communist secret agent in that town before the Chinese took it. He wrote first of all a lot of rude things about Britain and America and then came his main message. He told the Prince that the future of Tibet lay with the Chinese Communists. It was useless to think otherwise. This being the case, the very best thing for the Prince was to surrender as soon as the Chinese armies came in. One thing was clear Wanjee, the Communist, was still serving his Chinese masters. The Prince was disgusted. His orders from Lhasa were to fight and fight he would. It hurt him to receive letters like this from a 'traitor'. Was not Wanjee a Tibetan name?

Things were tense but because it was summer time and the weather surprisingly mild, the Prince thought, we could still have some fun. His plan fitted in, too, with a Buddhist 'cleansing' festival. He told his people to dam up a stream and make a large pool. They worked hard and in the end the water enclosed was six feet deep. He then had his servants pitch a couple of tents on the plain and we all enjoyed a time of swimming. The children loved it but however much they might laugh and play, the thoughts of invasion were always present in the grown-ups' minds.

After this little 'holiday', I was called away into the mountains where there had been a shooting accident. I rode out to the village concerned, with an armed nomad.

We kept a look out for bandits and once when a lone rider appeared, my nomad friend quietly loaded his rifle; but we got through safely. It was no joke in these wild parts. One of my Tibetan teachers had been cruelly shot by an enemy some twelve months before.

In the dark corner of a Tibetan house I was shown a man in great pain. He had a bullet lodged in the back of his knee. It was already three weeks since the accident had happened and he was very ill. I thought at first his leg was finished. The skin was as scaly as a lizard's. Talk about boys getting dirty, I had never seen such dirt on anyone! I studied my medical books carefully and prayed once again. I didn't want to cut any veins while trying to get at the bullet! I gave him a few injections around the wound, then cut open the skin. In went the forceps and after some time, I felt the scrape of metal. Sure enough the bullet was there. I got the forceps round it and although it was a bit messy, I managed to pull the thing out. The Tibetans in the house were astonished. I am thankful to say that the man lived and walked again.

This village marked my farthest journey into Tibet, a place I believe, where no one from the West had ever been. I left copies of the Gospels in the hands of the people and took my leave.

Just a few weeks after my return to Gartok, in came a rider very fast on his horse. The worst had happened. The Chinese Communist Army had forced the main crossing of the Golden Sand River and were pouring up the valleys and over the passes. It was the real thing. The invasion of Tibet had begun.

CHAPTER 7

Chinese Conquest

I WATCHED THE PRINCE as he stood reading the report. Heartbroken, he tossed the note to his Commander-in-Chief.

'We're finished!' he said. 'Eighteen hundred are over the river at Gora. If they drive hard, they'll be here by tomorrow!'

Given a little more time and fresh supplies of arms from Chamdo, the Prince had hoped to stage a battle on the Gartok plain and defend his fort to the finish. What this might have meant I dared not imagine — perhaps a siege of the town and then the whole place burned down over our heads! I left the Prince to talk with his officers. The butter-lamps burned on through the night. It was hard to sleep but God gave me a wonderful promise and this kept my heart at peace. 'Thy shoes shall be iron and brass and as thy days so shall thy strength be.'* I awoke and looked across the courtyard. They were burning official papers and servants were preparing to flee. Early next morning the Prince came to announce his decision and I felt my way was also clear. Whatever happened I would go right through the tragic circumstances with God.

'We are withdrawing our troops to the north,' the Prince told me. 'Get a supply of medicines ready and I'll have

* Deuteronomy Ch. 33 v. 25.

horses for you within the hour.' His men were nearly frantic trying to cram the Prince's treasures into boxes ready for the road. He looked at them and said sadly, 'What do these things matter now? We have lost our nation!' As the news leaked out that the Tibetan Army would abandon Gartok, law and order began to break down and many were tempted to loot and steal.

Another despatch came in. The forces at the river were completely routed. It was hopeless now. The Prince could picture his men dying in the mountains. Retreat was meaningless. He must act quickly to save lives. He could well have escaped but he rejected the thought.

'I must go and surrender!' he said. He was very brave. He seemed to value my friendship in this dark hour and my heart went out to him.

'Shall I come with you?' I asked, 'and act as your interpreter?'

He was surprised that I should risk my life. He thought for a moment, then said to me, 'Yes, come with me,' and we walked towards the horses saddled in the yard.

We rode, in silence, through the frightened crowds. 'Don't go! Don't go!' cried an old lama and took hold of the Prince's bridle, but the Prince rode on. The tinkling bells of the horses mingled till it sounded like distant pipes played mournfully amongst the trees. As we passed through the villages, folk were ready for the flight to the hills. It was like the day of a funeral. A nation was dying. It seemed too much for us to bear.

At one point the Commander dismounted and I wondered why. Out of the folds of his gown he brought some sweets wrapped in paper, a special treat, in Tibet. He gave us one each, then on we went again. It seemed a calm and kindly act in face of the increasing danger. From reports received, the Prince reckoned we should now be very near the advanced troops of the Chinese Communists. Any moment they might open fire. We were a sitting target and they would not know our purposes in riding out to meet them.

At last we stopped for we dare not travel further as a party. The Prince now chose a man and sent him forward to find out just how close the enemy were. Once again God had preserved our lives, for only a few hundred metres around the brow of the hill, he sighted the Chinese forces. They spotted him but did not shoot. Bravely he made contact with them and gave them the message from the Prince. We stood still where we were and in a little while were motioned forwards.

A local teenager from Batang was the first person to approach us. They did not send a Chinese soldier. The boy like many in that border town was able to speak both Chinese and Tibetan. That is why the Communists were using him. He looked up at the tall Prince and said the words he had been told to say. The Prince then bent over the young boy and spoke to him like his own child. The Chinese had pitched a tent in a field and the Prince and I were beckoned over and went inside to speak with their officers. Later in the evening the discussions were transferred to the upstairs room of a large Tibetan house nearby. There, by the light of burning pine-chips, the details of the surrender were worked out.

All fighting in South East Tibet must stop. The four or five hundred rifles in the fortress at Gartok must be handed over, and the Commander-in-Chief of the Prince's forces must return at once to Gartok, to make sure that all resistance to Chinese units advancing from other directions would cease.

The Prince, myself and his loyal men were now given orders where to sleep. The whole area was placed under

martial law. One false move and we would have been shot
by a sentry. The Prince and I were allowed to sleep in the
same room, so we talked a little of all that had happened,
then tried to get some rest. The next day we rode with the
Chinese troops over the mountains to Gartok.

Most of them were on foot, carrying guns and shouldering
their mortars. They wore yellow uniforms and on their caps
you could see the Chinese numbers 8 and 1, for it was on the
first of August, the eighth month, many years ago, that the
Chinese Communist Army was formed. Their name for it
was the People's Liberation Army. Over their shoulders,
like a long, thin sausage they carried a canvas bag. In this
was a mixture of flour, nuts, egg powder and salt which,
when mixed with water, made a kind of paste. It was full of
vitamins and kept the troops on the march in the high
altitude. Not every man could stand the fierce pace,
though; I saw one young soldier spitting blood. Any weak-
ness was soon revealed.

As I talked to their men I found that they looked at things
from a very different angle. We thought they were invading
Tibet. They said they were setting it free. They were obviously waging war yet told us they were fighting for peace.
The Prince had surrendered but they declared he had
staged a revolt against the Lhasa Government. They
painted the black situation white and made their evil deeds
sound like kindness. Wanjee, the traitor, was considered a
hero. I had never heard the like of it but their double-talk
was only then beginning.

Once outside Gartok they made the Prince get off his
horse and walk as the defeated leader of the Tibetan Army,
into the town. The Chinese staged a big victory parade and
showed off their modern weapons before the simple Tibetan
villagers. Through the archway of the fort they marched,
and once in command, lowered the Tibetan flag. A few

moments, and up went the Red flag of Communist China. It was hard to see it there, fluttering victoriously in the wind.

Back in the rooms of the fort, everything was deathly quiet. The Prince's three young children were safe in the care of their trembling nurse. How glad they were to see their father! They did not know that everything was changed and that he was really a prisoner in his own castle. The Prince himself despaired of the future. 'They will kill me I expect,' he whispered, but that was not their plan. They were craftier by far. The idea now, was to use him to control the people; to put their orders into his mouth and make the people obey him.

Gaga, my servant boy, turned up and had quite a lot to tell me. Someone had tried to steal horses after the Prince had gone but loyal people had caught the man and nearly killed him stuffing dung in his mouth. The magistrate next door, had run away but had later been attacked by bandits. Gaga was quite mystified by the Chinese. They had held a meeting for the local people and told them that they had come to free Tibet from the British and the Americans. As I was the only Britisher to be seen and the Chinese were everywhere, he couldn't quite get the point! At that time there were only two English people in Tibet — and no Americans at all!

It was dangerous now to move anywhere. Even in the fort if I went from one room to another I was liable to be challenged by a sentry. One day though, one of the Batang interpreters, a Christian who had been pressed into coming with the Chinese Army against his will, managed to slip a word to me in passing. It was amazing to see him. 'They say there is a spy in Gartok,' he whispered. I was thankful to him. It was his way of warning me of what was coming.

A few days after the occupation of Gartok, I was made to

appear before an army officer in the house of the magistrate. It was the same room in which we had held the three-day feast. Now like everything else in the town the Chinese had taken it over. 'You are to take your things over to a house in the village,' I was told. After this I was put in the charge of a young lieutenant named Chang.

Once back in my room I had to get everything packed up again so it was already late afternoon before I was settled into my new quarters. As I entered the room I found it full of Chinese soldiers. I was given a place to lie down and then told I could not go outside unless I went with one of them. The force of these words gradually dawned on me. They had made me a prisoner. A poor old woman saw my plight and brought me some milk to drink. The Prince bade me farewell and kindly gave me some silver money. It was a sad parting for us both with our future all unknown. So it was I lay down on my first night in captivity, little realising that more than eleven hundred evenings must pass, before I would be free.

CHAPTER 8

The Padlock Clicks

THE NEXT DAY WAS most trying. We were going. Then we were not going; and though we had expected to go, by nightfall somehow, we were still not gone. The Chinese Officer told me, I simply could not stay in the battle area so must go with some of his men to the rear headquarters at Batang. As the last rays of light were fading, I was made to stand with all my boxes in the big square of the fortress until the mules came.

The Chinese troops were singing the songs of their revolution. Then, as the stars began to shine, one of their officers spoke to them about the thoughts of their leader, Mao. To be a soldier in the Chinese People's Liberation Army is a hard life. You must not only do what you are told but you must think what you are told, whether you like it or not.

At long last the mules arrived and we loaded up. Gaga, who had been staying with a friend since my arrest, was made to come with us. He was a Tibetan through and through and hated being bossed around by the Chinese conquerors. We passed, in the dark, through a maze of sentries who seemed ready to shoot us at any moment. On all sides were the tents and campfires of the troops.

Chang, although in charge of us, had little or no idea of

camping. He kept us moving, on and on, into the blackness of the plain. Wherever was he leading us? The wind was getting up, and we could hardly see a thing.

'Stop!' he suddenly ordered, 'We will camp here!' It was, of course, 'madness'. We unsaddled the horses and I began to struggle with the tent. The canvas flapped wildly in the wind and the tent pegs were lost as soon as I put them down. The horses escaped and Gaga disappeared into the darkness. How he eventually caught them I do not know. We passed an uneasy night and awoke to utter confusion. It took us quite a while to reassemble and get away.

I felt heart-sick as we climbed the pass. At the top I took my last look at the plain. Away on the great horizon, I could pick out the ranges and the northern grasslands. I had hoped to tread that road but now I was being taken back a prisoner into Communist China. I could only cry out, 'Lord, you know everything! Lord, you know!' Then a verse from the Bible came to me and I began to feel better. It said, 'All things work together for good to them that love God, to them who are the called according to His purpose.'* I believed that, with all my heart, and received fresh courage to go on.

We stopped overnight in different villages, all of which were now in Chinese hands. After some days we sighted the Golden Sand River but Chang led us northward, this time, up its eastern bank to the place called Gora. This was where the main fighting had taken place and here and there wounded Tibetans were still to be seen. One poor man was lying in a vegetable garden. I was allowed to go over and tend to him. He had been shot in both arms and legs and countless flies were worrying his wounds.

We stayed at a house scarred by the bullets and I heard more details about the battle for the crossing. The Chinese

* Romans Ch. 8 v. 28.

had been very clever. Under cover of darkness they had put a small party of soldiers across the river at a lonely spot a number of miles further up. These daring men, unseen by the Tibetans, had landed on the western bank and had picked their way by night southwards over the mountains. Just before dawn they reached a position looking down on the village of Gora. At a given signal they opened fire. The Tibetans were completely taken by surprise and sent valuable men to deal with this unexpected attack from the rear. At this moment the Chinese on the eastern bank, jumped into their boats and rafts, and in great strength surged across the river and stormed up the beaches. Gora fell quickly. The losses were light and the first Chinese bridgehead in Tibet was thus easily established. The main Chinese setback occurred when one of their boats capsized and the troops on board were swept down the river. Very few were actually killed in the shooting.

That night, in the Tibetan house where Chang had put us, we heard what happened to the Commanding Officer of Hla Dun, who had been in charge of the fighting at Gora. It was all very sad. The Chinese had called on him to surrender but he would not give in. In the end they cornered him in a room in one of the houses. A Chinese soldier went in to get him out but the Tibetan officer shot him dead. Finally the Chinese managed to train a gun on him and kill him. It seemed impossible that the man who received us so kindly had died like this. 'Where is his body?' asked Gaga. 'I guess the dogs have eaten half of it,' was the awful reply. How dreadful war is!

Chang now led us down to the beach and on to one of the assault-craft used by the Chinese in forcing the river. On the other side, we spent a night on a rooftop. Chang got very strict and would not allow people to speak to me. We were getting nearer to the Communist Headquarters in Batang, and he seemed a bit nervous. He showed this the next day as we crossed the last pass, for he loaded his gun. 'One of our men was shot by a bandit, here, a week ago,' he explained. It was true, of course; the Chinese could take no chances for the Tibetans in the hills still did as they pleased.

When we entered Batang, I was taken first to one of the Christian Mission houses, now used as a barracks by the Chinese Army, where a soldier gave me a drink. Strangely enough, it was in a room where I had actually taught the Word of God in days gone by. It was hard to see these buildings occupied by men so opposed to the Gospel of Christ. Chang arranged for Gaga to stay in Batang but led me over to the big fortress of the town to be questioned by his Chinese Commander-in-Chief.

He was a young man for the high position, but his face was hard and his features narrow, a bit like a weasel's.

'What were you doing in Tibet?' he snapped.

'Missionary work,' I said.

'Who sent you?'

'God sent me,' I replied, making my words deliberately few. He looked at my passport. 'It is out of order,' he declared, though I doubt if he had ever seen one before. 'I believe you are a spy of the British Government.' He then asked what I thought about the war and I began to talk as if China and Tibet were two distinct nations. 'Two nations!' he exclaimed. 'Tibet is not a separate nation. It is part of China.' He was most displeased at my outlook.

'Take him downstairs!' he ordered, and Chang took me away.

Below the huge buildings of the fort we came to some dark cells that were just like dungeons. Chang looked at one and then said to the guard, 'No, don't put him in there. It's too dark.' There was still something human about Chang and I was thankful. Then we came to the next cell. It was nearly as dark as the first one, but a little light did reach it, so Chang said, 'Put him in there!' I stepped inside and immediately the heavy door was padlocked.

I heard it click.

CHAPTER 9

Some We Shall Execute

I PAUSED A MOMENT, then groped my way across the cell. There were no floorboards, just dust and sand beneath my feet. About a yard from the door I brushed against some wooden object. It was an old door, torn from its hinges and propped up as a kind of bed. There were two windows but both were covered with dirty paper. I peered through one of the holes, only to see a guard holding a gun with a fixed bayonet. I felt something very terrible had happened to me and I didn't know what to do; but gradually I grew quieter and was able to pray.

The days seemed very long and it was dark nearly all the time. I began to look forward to the guard coming with my meals which were mostly rice and very tough yak's meat. I was like an insect shut up in a matchbox. 'You haven't even got the freedom of a little dog,' said one of the soldiers. At night they lit a big red candle and the light and shadow danced like goblins around my cell. To me it was a horrible dream, and I couldn't wake up!

I still had my Bible, and on fine days, when a little more light came filtering through, I tried to read it, but even then it strained my eyes, and after three o'clock, it was largely impossible. Although I could wash a little every day, the dust began to affect my skin. How long could I last out, without falling ill? One day I asked Chang if I could possibly have a walk outside. God softened their hearts and I was granted permission.

Most days I walked up and down for an hour or more, between two soldiers. How lovely it was to see the hills again! How sweet the sunshine and the bright blue sky. The trees were turning to red and gold. It was the autumn time. It was all so beautiful. Whilst walking up and down one morning, Chang came out of the fortress and spoke to me about my future.

'I've got news for you,' he said. 'We've captured another Englishman, the radio operator at Chamdo.' This meant Chamdo had fallen and Robert Ford was also in their hands.

'And I tell you what we're going to do to some of you foreigners,' Chang went on. 'Some of you will get three years in prison and some of you ten. And what's more, some of you we'll execute!' I was rather shaken, for I knew he meant the firing squad.

'Whatever for?' I asked.

'Oh, for doing things against the people,' he said. 'You'd better start thinking what *you've* done against the people.' And with these words he sent me back into the dark cell.

Awful fears now rose in my heart. Would they really take me outside the city early one morning and put me to death? Why, my father and mother wouldn't even know where I died! How could my life be just snuffed out like a candle, in the back of beyond? In the next few months many thousands of Chinese folk were killed in this way. The Communists don't like to keep too many enemies; so I wondered what would happen to me.

Then I began to think of my Saviour. He was arrested and falsely accused. 'He makes himself a king!' the rulers

shouted. Then Pilate washed his hands and Jesus was taken
to be crucified. They had no guns in those days but they did
have crosses. How they mocked him and whipped him and
then at last hustled him through Jerusalem to the skull-faced
rock. He loved the people and cared for them but still they
executed him. It was for me He died.

Then as I thought of Him, my Master, something happened right inside me. One moment I was so afraid, cling-
ing to my little life and almost trembling, but suddenly He
had set me free. My hands unclasped. My fears were gone.
My heart was flowing out to Jesus. His everlasting arms
were round me. I knew He would not let me go. His peace
was mine. Whether I lived or died, didn't matter any more.
I felt like singing. And back into my tired mind there flowed
a song of boyhood days. I learnt it in my Bible Class. How
very real its meaning now:

> Out there amongst the hills my Saviour died.
> Pierced by those cruel nails,
> Was crucified.
> Lord Jesus Thou hast done all this for me.
> Henceforward I would live
> Only for Thee.

After this experience, God gave me great encouragements. One day when I was having my exercise between the
soldiers, I suddenly saw a sparrowhawk chasing a sparrow.
I was immediately caught up in the struggle. To be quite
honest, I thought of the sparrowhawk as being the Communists and myself as the sparrow. You can imagine how
happy I was, when the little sparrow escaped to the eaves of
a house nearby. I kind of breathed again. It was as if I,
myself had escaped. Then came to me the lovely words of
the Lord Jesus, 'You are of more value than many sparrows.'

It was very moving. If He cares for a sparrow as it dies, then how much more must He care for me!

On another day, not long after this, I saw an old man in the distance walking towards the courtyard. The public footpath ran close alongside but most people, whether Chinese or Tibetan, were afraid even to come near, let alone look, at a prisoner of the Communists. But, I had seen this old man before and knew him quite well. He was a dear old Christian and for many years had cared for the Church in that place. When he saw me he did not turn away but kept walking. In his hand he had a special stick. I remembered it because once, when I was in Batang, he talked to me about it. On the handle were carved the three Chinese characters, Faith, Hope and Love. 'When I feel sad,' he told me, 'then I look at these characters and they cheer me up.'

As he came across the empty courtyard, I thought the soldiers would run across and arrest him, but they did not move. He went right over to the other side, looked at the house where the sparrow had escaped and then, having decided what to do, turned and started to come back. Nearer and nearer he came. I could hardly believe it. Still the soldiers did not touch him. As the old man passed me, he whispered something in Tibetan. '*Samba me dug*,' he said; a simple message but such a help: 'Don't be down-hearted.' They did not arrest the old man that day but I wonder what happened afterwards, to this fine old soldier of the Cross, and one of the many brave believers in the Lord Jesus witnessing behind the Bamboo Curtain?

CHAPTER 10

Farewell to the Christians

ALMOST SEVEN WEEKS HAD gone by since I had been arrested and put into the dark and dirty cell. The first shock had now worn off and I was able to organise my day. There was the morning meal, some exercise and then, if there were sufficient light, the reading of the Bible. If the light was too weak, then I would recite passages of Scripture. I was glad for all I had learned in days gone by. At times I would make up poetry. Then about four in the afternoon I was brought my second meal. In the evening I would just sit and think and after a time of prayer, retire early to bed, by which I mean, lying down on the old door, in my sleeping bag.

The Communists viewed me very much as an enemy and almost certainly as a spy. From what was said, I learned that they were going to send me to Chungking, to the People's Court. Chungking was one of the biggest cities in western China and the seat of the Communist Government for the area. It all sounded very serious and Chungking, too, was very far away across the mountains. It was now December and growing colder. Batang was only 10,000 feet; if it felt cold in the town what would it be like on the passes?

One day I was given a treat, at least that's what it was to

me. It was nearly four months since I had had a bath and I felt really dirty! (Mind you, this kind of thing does not worry the Tibetans. They take about one bath a year, but then so might you if you lived in cold winds on the mountains and had no soap!) My hair too, was getting long, so my officer-in-charge decided I must be tidied up a little. I was given a haircut by one of the soldiers and then taken to a place of hot-springs a little way outside Batang.

It was like heaven walking through the fields with the sparkling waters of the stream beside me. The soldiers left me strictly alone and no one spoke to me but it didn't matter. I was so happy just to feel the rough path under my feet again and to let my eyes take in the wide expanse of country. At the hot-springs, I soaked and soaked in the warm sulphur-water. What a luxury! It was over all too soon, and then I had to go back to the fortress. The cell door opened and once again I found myself in the darkness and the dirt. I was like a bird returned to its cage. I'd had my little fly and now was back behind bars.

This time, though, I did not have to wait so long. Chang came to see me and explained what was going to happen. I had to get ready for a long journey over the mountains to Chungking. A party of soldiers would take me to Litang, one of the highest cities in the world, which was some ten days riding away. From there I would go to Kangting and then be escorted down to the Chinese Plains. It was all very exciting. I received orders that all my boxes were to go with me, so there was quite a bit to attend to during the next few days. On December the fifth we were ready to go.

Chang now introduced me to two new officers whom I had not met personally before. One was about forty, a very clever man named Chien, and the other was a younger man called Wang, who was very good with horses. Their job was to see me safely through to Chungking. Gaga, I am glad to say, was now allowed complete freedom and they let him return to his own village of Bo. I was permitted to give him various gifts for his services. This included one of our other horses but the grey was kept for me to ride on the forthcoming journey.

When the latter was finally brought in, I felt very upset at his condition. The Chinese soldiers had obviously worked him very hard. He had lost a lot of weight and there was a bad sore on his back. He just wasn't fit to carry me but there was nothing I could do. I would have to ride him. I felt a first-class animal had been 'thrown away'.

As I moved out of the Batang fortress with Chien and Wang, I could only feel thankful to my Heavenly Father for all His loving care over me in the big ordeal. It had been hard living in the darkness but nobody had hit me and I had not been shot. Chang had only been a lieutenant and had had his orders to obey. He dared not be too friendly for fear of what his Commander might say. When I thought of this I felt we had got through things not too badly together. They could have been so very much worse.

We now made our way through the narrow streets of the old walled city, the scene of many battles between the Chinese and the Tibetans through the long centuries. In my heart I had a special request which I longed to make to my officers. Plucking up courage I asked them before it was too late. 'Do you think I could say "good-bye" to the Christians before I leave?' Chien, the older man, felt that I could if I wished and allowed me to call at the home of one of my old friends, a very real lover of the Lord Jesus. His name was Timothy and he cared for the sick people in the town.

We knocked at the door and got a big surprise. It was twelve noon, yet on that particular day and at that unusual hour, practically all the active Christians in the town were gathered there. To me it was the over-ruling of God. They were naturally a little afraid of the Communist officers but Chien and Wang were quite easy about everything and remained in the room while we prayed. The great persecution of Christians in Red China was yet to come. So with loving farewells to these faithful servants of God, I turned again with my officers towards the road. Slowly we wound our way out of the town towards the windy passes, the air getting colder and colder, each step of the way.

CHAPTER II

An Eastern Stable

THE FIRST NIGHT OUT we pitched the tent in a Tibetan village only three hours riding from Batang, and took our food in one of the local houses. Chien and Wang were astonished at my appetite. One of the Chinese made a kind of spaghetti, called 'mien'. I ate more than anybody! What my officers did not realise was that I'd not had a square meal for several weeks. In the tent, which I shared with Chien and Wang, I could hear them talking as I knelt and prayed. Chien was explaining to Wang, who had not seen this before, what I was doing. The next two days we couldn't get going. The donkeys that had brought our loads from Batang had been sent back and we were still waiting for the yak, a kind of cow with big horns, very like our highland cattle. The time hung heavily upon everybody, so in the evening they had a little party in the Tibetan's home. Each person had to sing a song and I even did a folk-dance with the family, dressed up in my Tibetan gown! It was a good one too which I bought specially to wear when staying with the Prince. It was edged with beaver and lined with lamb-skins. What a change from the cell in the fortress! Chien and Wang seemed to thoroughly enjoy the whole thing.

The next few days were tough. Up and up we went into

the bitter cold and frost, until we were crossing the passes at about sixteen thousand feet. Chien gave me a good measure of freedom. I was even allowed to go and get water from a stream and to gather yak's dung for the fire. We climbed above the tree-line and the ice was so thick, it was hard to obtain water. The little streams were frozen almost to the bottom and when we did break through the ice, the water was muddy.

On one of the highest passes, the grey refused point-blank to go any further. When I dismounted he walked quietly on. As soon as I was on his back again, he would stand stock still. The whip would do nothing. His strength was gone. But then so was mine! The weeks in prison had made me weaker than I realised and I could hardly put one foot before another. It was also bitterly cold. Slowly, we edged forward, I with my two feet and the grey with his four. What a struggle, but at last we made the ridge. The gradient changed. We were over and going down. At night it was difficult to pitch the tent. The ground was so frozen that the iron tent-pegs bent when we drove them in.

By December the twelfth, we reached a broad desolate valley. We camped there that day but were almost blown away by a wind that swept like a hurricane across the flats. Our tent was held down by big boulders and it is a wonder it never ripped apart. Here we saw a great sight — a huge convoy of yak, about twelve hundred in all, bringing in supplies for the Chinese Army. Most of the rice was wrapped in skins and sewn neatly together, to make loads of about sixty pounds. Some of the Tibetans, when the Chinese weren't looking, would make a slit, take out the rice and fill the skins with earth! The Chinese had a lot of trouble in store, from this conquered but still defiant people.

We now began to cross the vast stretch of grassland that

leads into Litang. It was a wonderful experience to see the herds of antelope scattered across the plain. We stopped early and Chien organised a shooting party. They didn't let me have a gun, of course, but they did let me join in. The idea was to try and close in on one of the herds from different angles, then the man who found himself best placed would take a shot as they ran away. Wang tried fifteen times but still failed to get one. I could only be thankful he didn't hit me! If all the soldiers in the Red Army shot like he did the Communists would never win a battle. It was a hair-raising technique especially when you heard the whirr of the bullet whizzing past your ear. We were sorry not to get any fresh meat as we were living on very poor rations.

We reached Litang on December sixteenth. The lama city held three to four thousand monks and the ordinary city about two thousand people, but much of the population I believe, had dispersed to nomad encampments and distant villages in the country. I was taken at once to the old Government buildings which now were the head-quarters of the Chinese Army. To my great relief I was not put in prison, but allowed to be with the soldiers. Everyone was just about frozen stiff. There was a wind that went right through you and we spent most of the time huddled indoors around a charcoal fire, breathing in fumes of carbon monoxide!

We rested in Litang for about five days and then on December the twentieth, we took the trail eastward once again, heading for Kangting and Chungking. Within the first two miles we had a minor catastrophe. A whole basket of carefully prepared meat, a very important part of our supplies disappeared. It seemed a great pity.

One evening as we sat resting in the tent after the journey, we suddenly heard Wang, with an angry voice, swearing at one of the Tibetans. Chien looked at me and said, of Wang, 'That man has got no sense.' In a few moments, Wang returned and said heatedly, 'I've just found the fellow who stole our meat!' He was really mad about it. But I think Chien told Wang off because afterwards, they brought the Tibetan in and tried to smooth the quarrel over. What Chien knew and Wang had failed to realise was, that although the Tibetans handled the yak for us, they still hated the Chinese and they would easily get a knife in the ribs if they weren't careful!

The low temperatures continued. In my sleeping bag at night, tucked up inside the tent, I wondered what it must be like, standing on guard in a frost as cruel as that. It was my turn, it seemed, to be comfortable! We were always glad, I can tell you, for our hot drinks of tea, the only trouble being, that it look so long to boil it up, in that high altitude.

Before we broke camp one morning, there was great excitement amongst the Tibetans of our party. We looked across the valley and there on the hillside we could see deer again. As soon as they were sighted, the hunt was on. I did not join in but had a grand-stand view as the men scrambled all over the hillside, trying hard to bring one down. Again we failed so there was no stew after all.

The days slipped by and sometimes, along the road or at the camp-fire, I had opportunities to talk to my officers about my Saviour. My missionary efforts were still going on and I felt somehow that Chien, although a Communist soldier, respected me. He certainly trusted me greatly, and did his best for me and, this I felt was the kindness of the Lord. I might have had a real bully over me.

Eventually we climbed across a high and windy pass and down into a Tibetan hamlet with just two or three houses. We walked in through a courtyard to a doorway, which in turn led to a stable. As usual this was on the ground floor.

We clambered up the notched tree trunk which served as a staircase to reach the Tibetan family who lived there. Chien told the man that we wanted to stay the night and he showed us a place on the floorboards. Tibetans tend to sleep on the floor, not only in their tents but also in their houses.

We were all pretty tired, so after a meal we prepared to pack down for the night, but Chien told me to go and feed my horse before retiring. I climbed down the tree trunk and came into the dirty little stable. There were several animals there but I managed to find my horse in the growing darkness. The poor old grey; it was hard for him too. As I stood there quietly for a few moments, my mind went back over the days. I found myself trying to remember the date, just like I did at school, when the teacher told me to put it at the top of the page.

Then it came to me. It was Christmas Eve! I looked around. The stable was a wretched place. The smell of the animals filled the air, and straw and dung lay underfoot. What filth and squalor! Things suddenly came together in my mind. It was Christmas Eve and here I was in an eastern stable! My thoughts travelled back to that first Christmas Eve and that little stable at Bethlehem, where the Saviour was born. It was to a place like this He came, I thought. I forgot all about being a prisoner. I felt so thankful and full of worship. I had no gold, no myrrh, no frankincense to bring, but all at once that stable was a holy place. Jesus Himself was there. I gave the hay to my horse and climbed back up the tree trunk and lay down on the boards. I felt very near to my Lord that night, for Jesus we are told, had nowhere either, to lay His head.

Later on the words of a song we used to sing, away in England, came back to me. They somehow caught the meaning of it all.

Love to the uttermost, love to the uttermost,
Love past all measuring His love must be;
From Heaven's highest glory to earth's deepest shame
This is the love of my Saviour to me.

As the great missionary, Paul once said of Him, 'He is not far from every one of us.'

CHAPTER 12

Over the Edge

ON CHRISTMAS DAY WE moved downwards through a shadowy defile, where the sunshine never reached. It was icy cold and very still. Just before noon, having descended for two days, we reached the shores of the River Yalung, a big tributary of the Yangtze. It was two to three hundred metres wide. Huge piles of yak-hide rice bags were stacked along the beach waiting for more Tibetans and fresh yak to carry them into the plateau.

I was motioned forward to a small ferry, with the grey. We were to cross where two streams met beneath the sheer face of a towering rock. The waters looked ready to suck us under at any moment. As the animals were boarding the ferry, I realised that once again we were facing great danger. We launched out into the flow and almost at once were carried away. The horses were restless and shifted uneasily. God kept our lives safe. Any panic with the animals and we would have easily capsized. That river seemed as wide as the Atlantic to me, but at long last we reached the other side. We picked our way through the stones and mud and climbed up to the village of Yachiang, perched high on the hillside above flood-level. I gave some silver rupees to a local fellow to feed the grey; and we passed another peaceful night under a solid roof.

The next day took us through a perilous gorge, where the trail was only the width of a horse and rider and one stumbling step could have plunged both on to the rocks below. By about four in the afternoon the grey was at the point of collapse and we thought we would have to abandon it. A Tibetan suddenly appeared and offered to buy the horse, for next to nothing, on the spot. How they know horses! He must have realised that all it needed was care and feeding and it would be fabulous again. We held on to it, however, and after giving it maize that night, it regained some strength. The energy still left in the animal was surprising. When we gave it the food, it ungratefully lifted its hind legs and with a terrific lunge, all but smashed in the chest of a boy standing by. It was a narrow escape.

On December the twenty-eighth we reached a place called Ra Nga Ka which was the road-head for motor transport. Lorries and trucks from China brought in supplies to this point and then returned down country to the plains. Today the road goes right through to Lhasa, but at that time there was nothing but yak trails between there and India.

Whilst in Ra Nga Ka, who should pass through the village but Pangda. He had been to Kangting to talk to the Communists and now was on his way in, to discuss things with the Lhasa Government. Thus I had a chance to say good-bye to this old friend also.

Chien arranged for us to go by truck from this village, over the remaining miles into Kangting. The animals and the loads were to come on later. I carefully dressed the sore on the back of the grey before leaving. It was my farewell gesture of thanks to this faithful animal, so full of strength when we bought him but now just a shadow of his former self. I hope he found green pastures around Kangting, which at only eight thousand feet or so, was much less barren.

I had not been in a vehicle for over two and a half years so it was quite a novelty to be driven along, but whether four wheels would be any safer than four hooves remained to be seen! My fellow passengers were a number of Chinese soldiers sitting on the floor of the truck, but I preferred to stand and view the scenery. We went gaily along over hill and dale until we came to a steep incline and there the lorry began to falter.

Suddenly something in the engine slipped and in a matter of seconds, we were moving backwards downhill. There were some agonising moments as the driver struggled to regain control but he failed and the vehicle picked up speed and down the hill we went. If I'd been a kangaroo I could hardly have done better. Talk about the Olympics! With one terrific leap I jumped clean out of the truck, sailed through the air and landed safely on the ground. When I picked myself up the truck was gone. It had careered over the edge down a very steep bank and would have gone on and on to final disaster, if there had not been a more level ledge below. There it came to rest, all the soldiers still inside it. And there was I the prisoner, on the road, waiting to be collected!

Well, we all breathed again and took stock of the situation. At least the lorry had not overturned. After some tinkering around, they got the engine going again and by taking the truck a long way round, eventually got it back on to the road. Slowly we tried the hill. We crept along at a snail's pace and inch by inch we made the top. Now it was plain sailing, or at least we thought so; but if you need an engine to go up hill, you certainly need brakes to come down. This time it was one of the soldiers who guessed what was wrong and went in for 'the high jump'. I was standing at the wrong place so did not grasp what was happening. Lo, and behold, we were just about over again!

The drop this time was quite sheer but, as the brakes began to give, the driver just managed to slew us round against a stone and there we were, poised on a precipice and the edge of eternity.

We got the vehicle straightened up, then, keeping her in gear and using the tiny bit of brake-power left, we gently eased our way down the mountain. Then believe it or not, as darkness fell, we ran out of petrol! For the next few miles, where the road was less steep, the driver dared to coast a little but even he cracked under the strain! He managed to stop the lorry at last and leaving it where it was, refused to drive it any more. We walked in the pitch-dark to the outskirts of the city of Kangting, something of an anticlimax for the Chinese Army, who had brought me thus far but could take me no further; and yet a triumph for the One I served, who, in spite of every danger, had brought me safely to this town!

CHAPTER 13

To the People's Court

FOURTEEN MONTHS HAD PASSED since I was last in Kangting. At that time, half the people in the streets were Tibetans. Now there was hardly a single Tibetan to be seen. The Chinese had completely taken over. I was led away to a big house which backed on to a cliff. In this ramshackle old place I was kept a prisoner in a small room without furniture. The cold, bleak wind blew day and night through the tattered paper windows but one thing that made up for everything else, was the fact that there was electric light, and thus I could see to read my Bible and to write my diary. The house was full of soldiers and the place a bedlam of jabbering voices and constant footsteps. It was not exactly a rest-home for weary travellers!

One day at Kangting I was taken to some hot-springs like those outside Batang. Central Asia is a place of earthquakes, and this means that the molten lava which makes volcanoes is never far away, It is what the scientists call an area of 'thermal activity'. Where you get this kind of thing, hot sulphur water tends to come out of the earth. In backward parts of the world, where there is no hot or cold running water, these hot springs are very popular for bathing. In fact they are the only places where you can really get clean. As we were all rather dirty, we were very glad to go along and get freshened up after the journey.

Everywhere I looked, the old religious slogans of China had been replaced by the sayings of Mao and the Communist Government. They stuck them up everywhere. Nearly all the Chinese I saw were in some kind of uniform and I got the feeling that nothing could ever be the same again. The town was just like an ant-heap that had been disturbed.

On New Year's Day, the soldiers, who called each other 'comrade', had extra food. They loved these savoury meat dishes and gave me a portion too! Many of them were not much older than schoolboys and whatever Mao might teach about the greed of the rich, they still liked a good 'tuck-in'. Sometimes I met soldiers who had been on the other side and had fought for Chiang and the Chinese Nationalists. At some time they had been taken prisoner and after being retrained by the Communists, had had to serve in the People's Liberation Army. Now they were supposed to fight loyally for their new masters in West China, but they still looked back longingly to the old days before they were captured.

Even the children had been affected by the Communist Army in Kangting. One day two youngsters wandered in to my prison room, from the street. They were full of mischief, just like any other boys and girls, whatever their race. What made me sad, though, was that they began to joke and laugh about the Lord Jesus. They had in their hand a Communist 'comic' which put Lenin and Mao, the leaders of the Communist revolution in the place of God. 'Lenin is our sun,' it said, whereas the Bible makes it clear that Jesus Christ is 'the Light of the world' and the 'Sun of Righteousness'.

About the seventh of January, we piled all the baggage on to an open lorry, climbed on board and once again,

Chien, Wang and myself were on the road. We drove down the rocky valley until we reached the Tung Ho and the shaky wire-rope bridge, where the poor old Gebo fell through, that terrible night. A big new bridge was now being built by the troops. As it was not yet finished, we crossed the river on a ferry and after a night in the Chinese town of 'the twinkling lights', we drove over Two-Wolf Mountain. We had breathtaking views of Mt. Minya Gonka, rising majestically nearly twenty-five thousand feet, but when we crossed the next pass, we ran into heavy snow. This continued to fall as we entered the forests of the eastern slopes and was with us all the way to the lowlands.

Another day or two on the road brought us to the home-base of the Army Intelligence Unit to which Chien and Wang belonged. It was hidden away in a big Buddhist monastery. The temple courtyards were deserted now. It was a peculiar place to be a prisoner, and kind of eerie with all the big images and idols around. Knowing Chinese, I was able to understand some of the things that were being said around me. I was alarmed to hear that quite a number of local farmers had been executed by the firing squads. Chien and Wang had now completed their task. They had brought me down from the vast hinterland to their head-quarters. Things however were going to be hotter from now on. Step by step the Communists were getting rid of their enemies; and if I were their enemy would they get rid of me? Had not Chang said of us foreigners, 'Some we shall execute!' The news around me was not very comforting.

I now said good-bye to Chien and Wang, being handed over to another young officer who was to take me to Chungking. We drove through the province of Szechwan and it was good to see the green and rain-soaked country-side after the barren highlands of Tibet. I enjoyed the ride but the People's Court was uncomfortably near. We reached Chungking, the West China capital of the revolution, on January the seventeenth. It was now 1951 and my journey from Batang had taken forty-four days.

As soon as I arrived I was delivered to a detention centre, and put in a room alone, though it did have a little furniture, namely a rough sort of bed, a table and a chair. Its windows, however, looked out onto a wall of rock. Within minutes I was brought before two officers. One was a hard-faced man called Yang and the other, a younger man with an eye that refused to focus in the same direction as the other. I never got used to that eye. It always made his questioning more difficult to bear.

'You are aware of your position, aren't you?' he said. I did not know at first what they meant but I soon learnt. I was what they call 'an enemy of the people', that is to say, somebody who would not go along with the Communists. 'The people' referred to any who sided with the Revolution.

That night they came to my room and I was searched. They took just about everything away, including my Bible.

'Must you take my Bible?' I exclaimed. 'Surely I can keep that?'

'These things will be returned to you when we have finished with them,' they said. It was three years before I saw them again.

CHAPTER 14

The Thousands Die

Now THEY BEGAN TO question me. It all started off in a 'friendly way'. Yang looked in and said with a smile, 'Have you got enough to eat?' Other officials also looked in and we chatted away. Then came the big change. Yang returned one day with his face like thunder.

'You have lied to us!' he claimed. At first I felt angry; but it was no good. I must talk to these people. 'What about that letter you wrote to the Lhasa Government?' he said. I could see they would want to know every detail of my movements and all about our contacts in Tibet. It was going to be a hard time. The simplest act in their eyes would be viewed with suspicion.

As the weeks passed, I became very tired. I slept twelve hours some nights and this was a gift of God to me. The last three months had been so crammed with strain and excitement and this, together with the poor food and long journey, had begun to tell. These welcome hours of rest would strengthen me for the new pressures only now beginning.

On one occasion when the guard took me to the toilet, there was a security slip-up. I met another Englishman. Had the officer in charge got to know there would have been a proper rumpus. This 'foreigner' proved to be Robert Ford, the radio operator from Chamdo. He gave me a good wink and a smile and I knew he was holding his own, even though nothing was said. A day or two later one of the guards interested in English came with a scrap of paper on which was written a single word.

'What is its meaning?' he asked me. I told him and then casually turned the piece of paper over. On the other side was scrawled the following sentence. 'I translated a letter of Bull's to the Chamdo Governor. I should not have done this.' I had little doubt that this was Ford's way of telling me the kind of line he was taking with the Chinese and their questioning. It was becoming more and more obvious that all that George and I had done (or indeed, had ever hoped to do) to help the Tibetans, would be counted as a crime against the Communist regime. It never occurred to them that the big crime as far as Tibet was concerned was the way they had sent in their armies and conquered this helpless people. The Tibetans had at no time asked the Communists to set them 'free'!

Very soon I was moved to another building in a different part of Chungking. The windows were again covered with paper but here and there I could see out. I saw the sunset through one of these peepholes. I shall never forget the great ball of fire passing slowly down behind the hills. It reminded me of the great old hymn:

> *Though like the wanderer*
> *The sun gone down,*
> *Darkness be over me*
> *My rest a stone.*
> *Yet in my dreams I'd be*
> *Nearer my God to Thee!*
> *Nearer to Thee.*

My questioning often took place in a big room with

a huge window that looked out on a wide stretch of country sloping away to a river. The interrogators, that is the people who asked the questions, sat with their backs to the glass so I had the chance to look away to the horizon. This helped me very much, living as I did day and night behind four walls. The sessions were difficult although the questions were childish.

'You took photos of things in China and sent them to England,' they said accusingly.

'Of course I did. Any person abroad does that, but that was only to my family and my Church,' I answered.

'Yes, and then they could send them to the British Government!' The thing seemed quite ridiculous to me. I had never sent a photograph to the British Government in my life, nor had my friends at home.

'You took photos of the Yangtze River,' they insisted.

'Yes,' I said, 'but that was for the scenery.'

'But the river is of military importance! Surely you realise that? My, you've got a lot to learn. Once you view things from the people's standpoint, everything will look different to you.' (It certainly did.) 'You think what this involves,' they continued, 'taking photos of military objects and sending them to Britain? And that is not the only thing you did. You were always talking to Pangda and Rapga and giving them a bad idea of us Communists and our work. That is what we call rumour-mongering. It's the sort of thing you spies do, of course. And tell us, why did your friend George go to India?'

I knew that George had made his decision with great sincerity, hoping against hope that the Chinese Communist invasion of Tibet might be stopped and that the Gospel might be preached throughout Central Asia. But I did not feel, as yet, I could answer them in detail.

After much prayer in my room I decided the only way to

deal with these men was to be quite straight with them. I would speak the truth and leave the issues in the hands of God. This decision gave me great peace and I received fresh courage to go on. As a result for two days, they left me alone; but then my case started all over again.

I was pestered with military officials and civil officials, and they had me out for questioning in the daytime and at night. After a night session, one of them might come to me at seven o'clock in the morning and say, 'Ah, you haven't been sleeping very well. You must have something on your mind! You are afraid to tell us everything but you will have to in the end. Who was it in the British Government that sent you to Tibet? If you won't tell us, then we shall send you to a place where you will suffer "special bitterness"; and if, after that you won't talk, then without a shadow of a doubt, you will be shot!'

'If only you could see inside my mind,' I said to Yang.

'When we put a bullet in it, will be soon enough!' was the cruel come-back.

'What do you think?' he said, 'We have a nice gift from one of your friends.' Rather simply, I wondered if one of the Christians had sent something to me. 'It is marked, "Made in U.S.A.",' he gloated. I was at a complete loss to know what he meant.

'A pair of handcuffs!' he exclaimed gleefully. 'Your friend America sent them over here to put on our young people, so what better idea than to put them on you!' The deadlock was complete. I knew absolutely nothing about the British Government that would satisfy them, so if they kept me for twenty years, they would never be the wiser.

'Well, I'll give you just another two days to make a confession and after that, if you don't tell us everything, you'll go into that little room under the stairs, in chains and handcuffs.' It seemed to Yang, I was altogether at his mercy, but higher hands than his, still held me. Outwardly I was their prisoner but as Paul often used to say, I was 'the prisoner of Jesus Christ'.

Back in my prison room I lay on my bed and, as I did so, I heard the radio playing somewhere outside. It was a programme of Beethoven's music and sounded like a waterfall on a summer's afternoon. It was so soothing and I listened to it for a long, long time.

My punishment was not long delayed. I was taken out of my room and put into a very much smaller one, with hardly any space to move. It was not totally dark, however, and I could still see out through a few peepholes here and there. They did not, as Yang had threatened, put me in chains.

At that time China was going through a terrible time. I was told later, that four thousand people were arrested one night, in Chungking alone. The prisons were quickly overflowing. People in their fear reported on each other and children even reported on their parents. It was a witch-hunt unequalled in history. Anyone who had done or said anything against the Communists was expected to confess it. If you didn't and somebody told on you, you could easily be shot. Thousands of people died up and down the land and many cruel and wicked things were done. Some of the finest people in China were shot because the Communists held things against them and didn't want them to live. People called it a 'class struggle' but it was hell let loose. There was more than politics behind it.

Yang asked me once, 'What do you preach?' I said, 'That Christ died for our sins according to the Scriptures ...' Before I could finish the sentence he raged at me, 'We don't want that kind of stuff!'

And this is what is wrong with Communism and what is behind it too. It is what the Bible calls 'the spirit of anti-Christ'. Behind all their high sounding talk is a bitter hatred of God; and without God man is always in the dark.

Day after day the executions continued. Yang made me listen to the radio. There was a confused blare of human voices! It sounded like a football match. 'Do you know what that is?' he growled. I hadn't, of course, the vaguest idea. 'That's one of the big mass accusation meetings,' he continued. 'Tens of thousands of people are there and some of our enemies are up before the crowd. I tell you, everyone of them will be executed!' He sounded delighted. 'And what's more, if you don't watch out, we shall prepare a meeting like that for you. Fancy dying, cursed by all the peace-loving peoples of the world. If your body leaves China, you'll be a lucky man!'

Things were surely moving to a climax. Maybe quite soon they would take me out to die. Many by now must have been praying for me, for God still kept my heart in peace. I sat in my tiny room thinking about the Bible and praying, but not all the time. Sometimes I studied the insects. I found about six different sorts of mosquitoes and the spiders were fascinating. They did their preying too, but a different kind from mine! They were amazingly clever at catching the tiny flies on the ceiling. They didn't catch them in webs but stalked them like a cat does a mouse. I would wait a long time, then at last one would pounce. Is that what the Communists would do with me? At other times I would do a bit of maths or think back over a lovely holiday. I recalled my first visit to Switzerland when just a teenager. I could still remember the thrill when I first saw the snow-capped mountains.

This was the period when the night-questioning began in earnest. They would take me out of my room and lead me away downstairs. There they would stand me up and sit me down, barking their commands and keeping me going like a yo-yo! Yang was generally in charge on these sessions and what stormy occasions they were. It was no fault of his if I went quietly to bed.

As I sat on the rough couch that almost half-filled my prison room, I began to think what I would do if it really happened. Supposing one grey morning they were to lead me out to the firing squad, what in actual fact would be my plan? I didn't know how they handled such matters. Maybe they would blindfold me. Perhaps even give me an injection. What would I say to the soldiers? Should I preach or pray before them or do something else? Then suddenly it came to me. I would sing. Not that I've ever been able to sing very well! But I was ready to sing on such a day. I began to think of the hymns and choruses of years gone by. Yes, it was bound to be a grey morning but God helping me, my song would be,

> *Some golden daybreak*
> *Jesus will come.*
> *Some golden daybreak*
> *Battles all won!*
> *He'll shout the victory*
> *Shine through the blue*
> *Some golden daybreak*
> *For me, for you.*

To those who know the Lord Jesus as their Shepherd, the valley of the shadow of death is but the way into the house of the Lord for ever.

CHAPTER 15

Place of Chains

IT WAS NOW THE summer of 1951. I had been a prisoner about nine months and in spite of all the executions across China I was still alive. I was tired of their constant lectures which painted the Communists as the world's 'do-gooders' and the British as its devils.

'I suppose there are some decent English people around,' said an official rather rudely one day. I expect he thought he was being generous; then he added, 'But all the other nations learnt their evil ways from you!'

Usually they talked to me along these lines: 'You are just a young fellow and we quite understand your position. You were brought up in Britain at the heart of an evil empire and so you are bound to have mistaken ideas. You can't help it. But since you have been with us and had the opportunities of listening to the teachings of Mao, you can't pretend you don't know any longer. Now you must throw overboard all your past beliefs and accept what we believe. You ought to think of your future, you know, because, if after hearing "the truth" from us you stubbornly cling to your old ideas, then it just goes to show how wicked you are. China has plenty of rice but the Chinese people won't feed you for ever. Maybe we won't shoot you straightaway but if, after all your opportunities here, you refuse to come over to our side, then we *shall* shoot you one day.'

This was all part of what is called 'brainwashing' and they do it to all their prisoners, wherever they are captured.

It now became unbearably hot. All the windows of my cell were kept tightly shut and my body broke out all over in red and yellow pimples. I felt absolutely awful. All I could do was to sit in one place hour after hour. At long last they did open a window but even then the heat was still terrible.

During the last few weeks at this Detention Centre, they brought me a long list of questions to answer. I had answered many of them before but the last question was the main one. I was asked, 'What change has your mind undergone since you came in touch with the Communists?' In other words, 'Have you changed any of your beliefs yet?' I was determined to write the truth and tell them exactly what I thought. God silenced my fears and I began to write:

'When great nations built their empires some, as you say, acted like monsters and devoured other nations. But, if you Communists use your powers to drag the millions away from God and down to hell, then you are worse than all before you. You are like an evil germ eating its way into the souls of men.' When I had finished I sent the paper in.

For nearly two weeks nobody came to see me, except the guard who brought me my food. The guards never spoke to me anyway in that Centre, they were too afraid; so it was a long time with no conversation. Then Yang appeared. He said to me, 'You have insulted the Government again.' He was strangely quiet. If I had known what was going to happen, I need not have been surprised. On two separate days, I was allowed to have a bath in cold water. I had only had about three baths in nine months and the coolness soothed my fiery body. Then on July the seventh they came for me. I was whisked away downstairs into a waiting jeep at about half past six in the morning and driven out of Chungking into the country. My eyes looked eagerly around me at all I saw but whether the journey was to end in life or death, who could tell?

The soldiers at the wheel drove about ten miles, then turned off the main road on to a gravel track that ran into a range of hills. We approached a big quarry in which stood a new building. I noticed at once it had long lines of windows, and every one was barred. The men inside it had built it. It was the Number One prison for people opposing the Revolution.

The jeep came to a halt at the head of a driveway leading down to the big entrance. I was told to step out on to the roadway. My heart sank within me. Coming up from the prison I saw a man being led by a Communist soldier. I was utterly horrified. On his ankles were thick, heavy chains. The links were so large that he could only shuffle along. His wrists were also bound by a strange kind of handcuff, a single circle of steel. 'And where are they taking him?' I fearfully pondered. Once inside the prison and past some men with guns at the door, I had to appear before the Governor. He and Yang made it clear that I had now come to the place where I must suffer 'special bitterness'. They said I had refused to tell them what I knew and now I was here in this prison with only myself to blame.

A guard led me away down the long corridors. Men were moving about doing various duties, in shorts and bare feet. Some of the prisoners were like the man I had seen, in chains and handcuffs. At the corners of the corridors stood soldiers in pill-boxes, their guns at the ready. I was taken to Cell 9 on the top floor. The room was not too small and had two windows with seven bars in each, letting in the light. There were floorboards and it was reasonably clean. The door was locked behind me and I took stock of my surroundings. The first thing I was conscious of was the kindness and mercy of God. This place although it looked like a chamber of horrors, was nevertheless cool, being situated in the hills. Within a few days my rash was gone and the sense of renewed health cheered me tremendously.

At Batang I was kept prisoner in the dark. Here I was kept in the light all the time. The electric light bulb in the ceiling burned the whole night through and the guards watched us at intervals throughout the whole twenty-four hours. There was no privacy at all. The electric light bulb was surrounded with wire. This was to keep prisoners from electrocuting themselves. In addition a prisoner with spectacles often had them taken away lest he cut his wrists with the glass. Two years in this big prison made me understand why these precautions were taken.

My first meal was brought by two Japanese prisoners still held by the Chinese since World War II. Five years had passed and their case still wasn't settled. Things didn't look very hopeful for me. After the Japanese prisoners had gone, I sat down on the floor, gave thanks to God who had kept me to this hour and so settled in to my life in the prison. In the first period of my imprisonment I had eaten meat most days of the week. After a while I had it twice a week. In the end, I only had meat once a month. Apart from the meat I had rice or steamed bread plus vegetables, but nothing sweet. I only had about half a cupful of sugar the whole three years I was in their hands.

That night as I was kneeling beside my sleeping bag, my prayer was rudely interrupted by the fierce shouting of the guard. I took no notice and went on praying. After quite a while there was the sound of more footsteps and a senior officer pulled back the bolt and walked in. He told me to lie down. Prayer, he said, was not allowed in the prison.

Another time, I was discovered praying lying down; then the guard made me stand up. 'Don't you know,' he said, 'there is no religious freedom for people like you?'

CHAPTER 16

A Voice from Below

DURING MY FIRST WEEKS in this sad place, Number One prison, I found it hard to understand what was happening. Not all the sounds made sense. Sometimes a party of prisoners in the courtyard could be heard singing. At other times there was a lot of jeering and shouting. Once I heard a man scream. All day there was the sound of men saying, 'Bow Gow'. This was the Chinese phrase for calling the attention of the guard. There was very little that a prisoner could do in that prison without asking permission. At a similar prison in Chungking, a prisoner told me, you could not even turn over at night unless the guard allowed it. We were not so strictly controlled as that, but even so, there was no going to the toilet unless the guard let you, and at night this was especially difficult.

The Governor explained one day the idea behind all that went on. This prison, he began, is really like a hospital. You prisoners have been poisoned in your minds by wrong ideas. We officials are like doctors and the guards are like nurses. The books we give you (and there were plenty of them) tell you the cure. This literature you study and the chains on your feet, are our treatments. We want you to be politically healthy and to play your part in the building of New China. When I heard these words I felt as if I were in a mental hospital where the lunatics were in charge and the sane were in straightjackets. Everything was upside down in this mad, mad world. I began to look at the books they supplied. Medicines! Treatment! It was like taking a fatal dose of drugs.

When I leaned against the cell wall one day, I could hear the prisoners in the next cell were not exactly enjoying themselves either. One poor man was crying out, 'They are going to execute me! I'm going to be shot!' Then I heard a man next to him say, 'Don't give up hope! Don't give up hope!' But after a while I thought I could hear another voice. This time, though, the sound was not coming through the wall but up through the floor. When the footfall of the guard had grown fainter, I put my ears to the floorboards and listened very carefully. To my surprise, I could hear someone singing, and singing in English. Gradually I managed to catch the words. It was not some popular number nor a revolutionary song like the men sang in the square. It was a hymn about the Son of God. I caught the chorus quite clearly:

> *Onward Christian soldiers*
> *Marching as to war,*
> *With the Cross of Jesus*
> *Going on before.*

I'd not heard the name of Jesus in English for a very long time but I was hearing it now. I began to sing back, softly at first, then louder and louder. We established contact. It was Robert Ford of Chamdo. Later on there was such a fuss! We were separately, and severely questioned over a period of three weeks. They said it was a terrible thing to think that two British 'spies' should be in touch with each other in a Communist prison!

At this prison in the hills my case was re-opened as if I had never been asked a single question before. At the point of a gun I was taken, time without number, to different buildings in the prison grounds. Under the glaring eye of a guard I would be made to sit on a stool just a few inches high. In front of me there generally loomed a high black bench at which the interrogators sat. Behind them very often, were larger-than-life pictures of Mao and other famous leaders of the Revolution. My 'treatment', to use the Governor's word, was very prolonged. I must have been questioned two or three hundred times.

The loneliness was just about breaking me now. I felt I was forgetting things, especially the words of the Bible. I looked afresh to God and a little poem began to form in my mind, like a prayer. It expressed my feelings and my fears:

> Let not Thy face grow dim, dear God,
> Or sense of Thee depart.
> Let not the memory of Thy Word
> Burn low within my heart.

How much longer I could go on I did not know. I had now been almost twelve months alone. The minds of some men in the prison began to be affected. To keep myself from going mad became a major concern. One poor man lived in a bundle of rags in a cell all on his own. One day he let out a piercing cry. He had tried to drink some water that was only for washing. The guard, quite correctly, stopped him but something in the man suddenly seemed to snap. 'You won't let me drink water!' he howled, in a high and broken voice. 'You won't let me be executed! You won't let me commit suicide!' It still haunts me, the agony in that scream.

Thank God he knows how much his children can endure.

Just at the time when I felt I was nearing my limit, an official took me into another room and asked me, 'Well, what do you think about your case?'

I did not waste words. 'Do just what you like!' I said. It was a strange thing to say but he took me at my word.

CHAPTER 17

God's Hold of Me

SOME SHORT WHILE AFTER this, I was sitting, as usual, all on my own, when a man with big goggly eyes and wearing a blue silk jacket was led into my cell. The official who had so recently asked about my feelings, was the person in charge. I came to know, in due course, that my new cell-mate ('fellow-student' was the Communists' word) was called Changli. He was a radio expert, a rather dangerous occupation in times of revolution. In quick succession, the official brought in other prisoners to join us until there were about half a dozen of us sitting round the room. The prisoners came from all walks of life. Some had served the Nationalist cause in various ways. There was also a university lecturer, a journalist and later on, a pilot of a Yangtze river-boat.

I thought this development was going to be helpful. At last I would have someone to talk to. Gradually, however, I found out that some of these 'fellow-students' had already gone over to the Communists' side and were put with me for a purpose. Changli and I were the odd men out. On the wall was hung a copy of the prison rules. These we had to learn by heart. Some were quite funny if you still possessed a sense of humour. One said, for instance, 'You must keep quiet. You must not peer round corners or gaze through windows. You must not speak loudly, sing, quarrel, spread rumours, whisper in twos, or talk to yourself.' Another showed up the evil side of the prison. It said that every prisoner had the responsibility to report to the Governor on what his cell-mates said and did; and this even applied to their thinking. In other words we were expected to spy on our fellow prisoners and this was greatly encouraged by the authorities, as one of their methods of mind-control.

The prisoners in our cell, who had confessed to doing or saying things against the Communists, tried hard now to make Changli and me confess too. The officials told them that if they could only break us down, then maybe they would get out of prison sooner. This was called 'helping'. The idea was that Changli and I were in danger of being executed or given long sentences, so if the other prisoners could make us confess something, then we might not be punished so severely. That's where the 'helping' came in. The result of this system was that you couldn't trust anyone. I found myself, if anything, more lonely than before.

Changli had got to the point where he didn't care what he said. He even mocked the officials with his replies.

'You are one of Chiang's secret agents,' they accused him. 'You were in touch with Taiwan on your radio.'

'A secret agent!' exclaimed Changli. 'Of course! I'm a secret agent, my wife is a secret agent and so are all my children. We're all secret agents!'

This made them really angry. When they threatened to shoot him, he dared the guard to do it. 'Go on, shoot me now!' he said. But, of course, the case was not yet settled and the guard could do nothing. It was all very tragic but had its amusing side. In the end they put him in heavy chains and a tight handcuff. He had to sleep in them and when he had a cold he couldn't blow his nose. The iron links bit into his ankle and although they did give him some medical treatment, he suffered horribly.

The time came when the officials set the other prisoners against Changli in a special series of what they called 'struggle meetings'. They were to struggle with him, not with their hands, but with their words and thus try and get his 'crime' out of him. They shouted and swore at him and gave him no rest. He had hours in the court and hours on the cell floor. They treated him as if he were the worst criminal on the face of the earth. Personally I doubt whether he had done anything worthy of imprisonment at all. For almost a whole week they would hardly let him sleep. Then they began to take down the things he said. He was almost 'crazy' by now. In Communist newspapers they sometimes talk about voluntary confessions. I was beginning to see how this was done behind the scenes.

Soon it was my turn for the 'struggle meetings'. They were very terrible although not so severe as Changli's. We were like a lot of spiders in a jam jar, thrown together to fight it out.

Every day we were supposed to learn more about the teachings of Marx and Mao. Marx was a German and the founder of Communism. Mao is the Chinese politician who has applied these ideas to China's problems. Sometimes I declared to the prisoners what God tells us in the Bible. Then the prisoners who sided with the Communists got very angry. They called me the dunce of the class and blamed me for holding back their progress; but I was a Christian and knew I could not accept the teachings of Marx and Mao. So I was taken out of the cell and given quite a lecture by the official-in-charge.

'This is a prison,' he said. 'You simply aren't free to speak about the Bible here. This is not a Gospel Hall!' I went back to the discussion amongst the prisoners. It was becoming more and more difficult. If I mentioned the name of Jesus, then some prisoner would shout against Him just to show how Communistic he'd become.

Over these months I became more and more worn out. I grew thinner and thinner and my mind more and more tired. I was always being criticized, always being told I was a bad person, always being ragged and nagged by the officials and the other prisoners. In my forehead I began to get a pain which would not go away. When people spoke to me, I started to blush. They tried again and again to destroy my faith. I began to feel I was changing. Since my arrest in Tibet nearly three years had gone by. I wondered how I could survive or hold on to God anymore.

Apart from matters discussed in the Communist newspapers, I had no news of the outside world. I did not know that Mt. Everest had been conquered or that Queen Elizabeth the Second was on the throne. By my third year quite a number of prisoners had been moved out of the prison to 'Reform through Labour' camps. If they had confessed a crime and accepted the Communist teaching, they were sent to a camp where they were supposed to learn the meaning of hard work. 'This,' they were told, 'will help you to understand how ordinary folk earn their living.' The strange thing was, that many of these prisoners *were* ordinary folk and *had been* earning their living before the Communists came and interfered with them. It wasn't just the rich people who were behind bars by any means. It was all very peculiar.

Once one of the officials came to our cell and pointing to three prisoners said, 'You! You! And you! Roll up your bedding!' The colour just about drained from their yellow faces. You see, they did not know whether it was for execution, a labour camp, or release. One man's case had been going on for four years without a verdict or a sentence.

If you gave up and refused to answer them, they might leave you for months on end until you spoke again. No one was allowed to view themselves as innocent. All the cases were held in secret. There was no open court-room attended by the public. There was no jury or counsel to help with their defence. There was no cross-examination of witnesses as we understand it. The officials simply said, 'We have evidence that you have opposed us. Now tell us what you said and did. The eyes of the people are "far seeing". If you hide anything it will be the worse for you. We know more about you than you realise.'

They would keep men for years. Husbands disappeared. Fathers were taken from their children. Women also were put in prison. Such people are not allowed to be in touch with their families until they are well 'reformed' in Communist thinking. It can lead to divorce. I actually witnessed a man pressurised into divorce for solely political reasons. You must not hold your wife back they said. You are a 'backward person' in the new society. Your wife in 'freedom', is going forward with the revolution and is busy building New China. You should let her go. How can you expect her to hold back for you. In the end he did what the officials wanted and signed the paper. As for myself, they never let me write to my parents even once. Nor did they let me receive a single letter, though my mother wrote to me every two weeks for three years.

By now many people had died before the firing squads and the 'enemies of the people' who were left were taught the teachings of Mao and then forced to work. The 'Reform through Labour' camps were just another name for slave-camps. China was corrupt, of course, before Mao took over. Then it was possessions men were after; now it is position. If you are not well-in with the Communist Party you have no real future in China. Of course there are all sorts of things being done for 'the people', as they say. There are new railways and roads; there are factories and better health services. They are trying to control the rivers and improve the crops. But even so, thousands are still happier to live in a shack in Hong Kong under the British flag and know that they are free. The Communist Government in China controls all the newspapers, the radio, the schools, and the universities. In factory, office, street and college they have Communist Party members spying and reporting. Their magazines always show their people smiling and laughing but I saw their agony and shared their tears.

An official who spoke to me at this time, without realising it, gave me one of the biggest encouragements I ever received behind bars. He said in a grumbling tone of voice, 'Your Chinese is improving but your mind isn't.' By that he meant that I was still a 'dunce' in their 'learning'; I had made no real progress in the Communist teaching. Thank God for that! What they did not realise was that Christ, my Lord, was living within me. He was keeping my mind in His truth. They could have changed me a thousand times but they could not change Him, for He was greater in my heart than the devil at work in theirs. They just couldn't understand it. They thought they were so good at their brainwashing and here I was a kind of 'blot' on their record! Maybe on account of this, or for some other reason unknown to me, I was sent in my last year, to another prison in Chungking.

There, in a gloomy cell, I was put with just one other prisoner. We sat much of the time in quietness as we were not permitted to do much talking. My cell-mate had bad eyesight and as his glasses had been taken away to stop him committing suicide, he had a really hard time. The prison was quite terrible. In the cell next to ours, men were shouting and raving at each other in some kind of 'struggle meeting'. You would think they were demon-possessed.

I begin to think about the Lord Jesus and my trust in Him, which the Communists had done everything to destroy. My mind was so tired now, yet deep down in my heart, I knew I still believed that Jesus was the Son of God; I still believed He died for me; I still believed God raised Him from the dead. Like Paul on the doomed ship, I could testify, 'I believe God! Whose I am and whom I serve.' I was weak but Christ was my strength. I came through sane and believing, not so much because of my hold on God but because of God's hold on me. What is a Christian? A Christian is someone into whose heart Christ has come to dwell. I had the Eternal in my heart. My mind therefore could never be destroyed.

I waited quietly for God to work. Prayer was winning. The Chinese tiger might bare its fangs but God, Himself, would claim the prey.

CHAPTER 18

When Iron Gates Yield

ON NOVEMBER THE ELEVENTH, 1953, my chief interrogator called me into the Court Room, gave me a severe lecture and then told me I was going to be sent out of South West China. I was puzzled at this and wondered where I was to go. Could it possibly be to the capital, Peking? Or was this just their way of saying my case was soon to finish? The chief interpreter also spoke to me. He put things differently. He said that it was not possible to settle my case in China but that once the Communists were in control in Britain, then it could be re-opened there. It was all very mysterious, but it was quite clear something was going to happen.

Then on December the second, an official discussed the question of my baggage. Finally on December the eleventh, the Governor of the prison, came in person to my cell. He led me past the guard with his gun and away upstairs to another Court Room, which I had not seen till then. On the way there were men with cameras, who took my photograph. Why was I suddenly 'important'? On a black table everything was set out. Officials with solemn faces sat behind it and a sealed document lay in front of them. If I were for the firing squad, it could not have been more serious. At last the moment came. They announced my sentence. I understood the Chinese and as the words were stated, a great relief swept through me. They were inflicting the biggest disgrace Red China knows: 'You are to be expelled from the People's Republic of China, immediately and for ever, for crimes against the Revolution!'

I was now marched straight downstairs, searched for the last time and then taken, with my bedding roll, to a boat on the river. Two guards were appointed to watch me and I slept with them on the open deck. I was handed back my Bible and my watch. All else was left behind. The guard in charge whispered something in my ear. 'You know the result of your case, don't you?' he said. 'We'll not handcuff you. Just you behave yourself and you'll be all right!' But two of their own people in our party, being taken to a prison down river, were handcuffed. Needless to say, I behaved very well. I felt I was dreaming. Day after day we sailed down the Yangtze, passing swiftly through the great gorges, until at last, we reached Hankow.

There I was transferred by my guards to a railway train and our long journey southward, through Central China, began. The carriages rattled on through the tea-plantations and the paddy-fields for thirty-six hours until the next day at sundown we drew near to Canton. Here my guards had to show my papers to the local police. All was in order and eventually we boarded a train bound for the Hong Kong frontier. Every minute now brought me closer to freedom. I looked out of the window at the banana palms, the paw-paw trees and the fields of pineapple. I had come from the frozen wastes of Tibet to the tropical shores of South China. At just before two o'clock, the puffing-billy of a steam-engine ground to a halt before the barbed-wire barrier. I walked with my guards down the length of the platform. A Chinese woman wept bitterly as we passed, throwing herself about as the Chinese do when very upset. I wondered if she had been turned back from the border. It was my last view of Red China — a woman in tears. Now I stood at the little gap in the barbed-wire. A bridge stretched across the river. It was a day of glorious sunshine and I could see the Union Jack fluttering in the breeze on the farther side. Suddenly the last command was given. I took a few steps forward and I was free. It was the nineteenth of December, I was told. I had been over three years and two months in Communist hands.

Within half an hour I was on another train being taken to missionary friends in Hong Kong. It had been a long hard road from Gartok to this bustling port of the Orient, but the God who never fails had brought me through.

That night in the home of my friends, I opened my Bible again. Its words were so reassuring after all the brainwashing of the years. 'I will destroy the wisdom of the wise,' God said, 'and bring to naught the understanding of the prudent.' Marx and Mao were passing away. Jesus alone remained. The next day, although rather weak and dressed in a borrowed suit, I was able to worship once more with fellow-Christians. As I regained strength I walked in the hills, drank in the mountain air and looked away wistfully to the farthest sea. I picked a sweet green leaf and held it between my fingers, till tears came into my eyes. My release was announced on the B.B.C., and a telegram came from my parents.

It said very simply, 'Well done, good soldier of Jesus Christ!'